we are the poors

WE ARE THE POORS

Community Struggles in Post-Apartheid South Africa

ASHWIN DESAI

MONTHLY REVIEW PRESS

New York

Publication of this book was made possible by a generous grant
from the Lipman Miliband Trust

Library of Congress Cataloging-in-Publication Data

Desai, Ashwin.
  We are the poors : community struggles in post-apartheid South Africa
/ Ashwin Desai.
      p. cm.
  Includes bibliographical references and index.
  ISBN 1-58367-050-5 (pbk.)
    1. South Africa–Economic policy. 2. Poor–South Africa. 3. Blacks–
South Africa–Economic conditions. I. Title.
HC905 .D38 2002
305.5'69'0968–dc21

                                        2002006897

MONTHLY REVIEW PRESS
122 West 27th Street
New York, NY 10001

Printed in Canada

10 9 8 7 6 5 4

contents

introduction

THE STORY TOLD IN THIS BOOK begins in Chatsworth—a township on the outskirts of Durban, the largest city on the eastern seaboard of South Africa. It describes an ongoing spiral of struggle against market-driven measures to make residents of poor communities become paying customers in a capitalist society supposedly made non-racial by the defeat of apartheid and by the embrace of the free market in its place. This struggle has spread from Chatsworth to other poor communities around Durban, and to other parts of South Africa. To say that this struggle begins in Chatsworth is a kind of shorthand, which saves the trouble of explaining each time that, like all revolts that grow, it has many beginnings. It could surely have been traced back to other sources. Even so, there are good reasons to begin in Chatsworth.

When I started writing this story, Chatsworth was both a place and a struggle. It should become apparent as the story unfolds that Chatsworth has also become a politics. Race and class, the old chestnuts, still loom large. But new political variants have emerged, happily immune to infection by Robben Islanders, exiles, and ethnic entrepreneurs; the ruling post-apartheid political faction. Unemployed, single mother, community defender, neighbor, factory worker, popular criminal, rap artist and genuine ou (good human being). These constructs have all come to make up the collective identities of "the poors."

The struggle in Chatsworth helped to ignite rebellions in other areas, and to illuminate struggles already happening elsewhere. These struggles, at first conducted in isolation from each other, have begun to jump the firebreaks of race and place. Will they continue to do so, and incinerate the fetters of old political allegiances and class compromise that have so immobilized us these last ten years? Or will the multitude be confined to the outer reaches of society doused by brigades of politicians, past masters of turning on and off the taps of struggle and expectation? Or will they stand side-by-side and in so doing light the way to a new society?

THESE HIDDEN STRUGGLES HAVE BEEN EPIC, because they have taken guts and imagination. Above all, before a new basis of solidarity could emerge, the ethnic handicap had to be overcome. Chatsworth itself was created as a dumping ground for people classified as Indian by the apartheid system, and most of the people who live there are Indian. This made participants vulnerable to race baiting. They were Indians dissatisfied with an African government. As events have unfolded, it has become apparent that this ethnic dimension has been a blessing. It bestowed upon people crude accusations from desperate politicians. These accusations, the people considered and then rejected with the formulation of counter-identities. As these upsurges have spread to African communities like Mpumalanga, colored communities like Wentworth and Tafelsig, so these new identities have been strengthened and attempts to divide-and-rule are met more with laughter than concern.

The visible part of these struggles, mass mobilization, began hesitantly. To grow, they required political and organizational innovation. Community leaders were marked with the labels of agitator, radical, and counterrevolutionary, used interchangeably. It was difficult to respond. Memories of past traditions of resilience and resistance had to be filtered through new buzzwords and adapted to changed conditions. The easy moral satisfaction of the anti-apartheid struggle was absent. Petit bourgeois support was slim and legal aid and foreign funding unheard of. Against a new democratic government, different boundaries to struggle had to be observed and, when breached, then breached with force rather than violence.

Remarkable political aptitudes developed. Linkages with niche allies, in hundreds of little engagements, were supremely expedient. The enemy was mocked, praised, lobbied, fought, voted for, slandered, borrowed from, set-up, debated, and chased away. All principle flowed from the need to ward off evictions, water disconnections and the like. No bridge was unnecessarily burnt. However, this instinct for survival also meant that concessions were made and public pronouncements could become politically murky.

Cultural and religious innovation, too, played a role. People cast about for theologies they could put to work. Religious ceremonies were decoded and given very contemporary moral force. In this way, hip-hop, bhangra, and the festival of (no) lights (Diwali) shared a platform, receiving applause and militant acclaim. Local icons were born with extensive reach into a youth subculture that ran on attitude rather than ideology. And for the "ordinary" people, the residents with biographies disfigured by poverty, it was discovered that no speech, workshop, or meeting could heal old wounds as healthily as did the labor around the now ubiquitous communal cooking pot.

History also was drawn upon to generate the charge necessary to keep the politics of the poor alive. Having pride of place in many a home in Chatsworth or Isipingo, there are photographs of grandparents as slaves and parents as sweat-shop workers. In these places people take pride in the knowledge that a moral giant, Gandhi, whose creed was anti-imperialist, once lived among them. Then there are memories of the student militants, the bombmakers, the unionists, the intellectuals of the struggle who showed how resistance to oppression could be forged. The ringing question carries its own sharp answer: is this what they fought for?

These struggles have taken place against the grain of every political party. People came to see that lobbying and due process was a futile fob-off when live ammunition was fired at them while they were begging for just thirty minutes more to obtain a court order preventing their eviction. Although tragedy constantly haunts those who operate in Chatsworth, the heavy- handed response of authorities has been a blessing. It has founded a politics that is unrepentant and unusually clear. In short, the struggles described here had to face the huge obstacle of fighting against those who wore the mantle of liberation—the African National Congress (ANC), in the first place—and thus had to undertake the task of forging very new weapons of liberation.

IT IS WORTH DWELLING ON THIS DIFFICULTY. At first, communities were slow to respond to evictions and water and electricity cut-offs. Their protests were not driven by ideology but by the need to survive and the desire to live decently. Initially, action took the form of pleas for mercy in the knowledge that this was a liberation movement in power. But the response was that payment had to be made. This was the policy, they were told.

The prestige and power of the ANC was such that many felt it was impossible to oppose their policies, or that opposition could only be couched in terms of loyalty to the vision of the ANC itself.

Many readers of this book will be familiar with the dramatic change in government in South Africa during the 1990s. In 1994 the ANC stepped off the back of a popular trade union and community-driven revolt against racial capitalism and into power. The revolt against apartheid had been bravely militant, resolutely socialist, and waged with the support of progressive internationalists around the world. The price of its triumph was paid in blood and broken childhoods. The conviction that all this suffering would be redeemed was affirmed at every surging funeral and in the sweat, beer, and tears that drew people into each others' arms at the end of every back street jazz concert. Every teenage struggle poet promised that the blood would water the tree of freedom.

The multitude was a network of rivers. Rushing out of schools, factories, and universities. Parting, joining, growing. It crashed through every wall the system had ever built. It ate razor wire, hit the police straight back, refused the chief, looked the future straight in the eye. The farmer's fences were now just wire and the soldiers were just scared teenagers. Anything could happen when one was between the broken and the built. The cities were shaking with our feet. Even white teenagers had learned to burn.

But this revolt had a flaw. The multitude that brought down the apartheid regime had a millennial faith in the exiled and imprisoned leadership of the ANC. The multitude that brought that ANC to power with millions of acts of rebellion, from strikes to burning barricades to refusing to stay and pay and obey, became a (just slightly fractious) people under the ANC.

Before long, democracy was more or less stifled within the ANC and its Communist and trade union allies. People that couldn't be bought were marginalized. It soon got to the point where you could get expelled from the South African Communist Party for advocating Communism. Once the conservative nationalists had cemented their hegemony within the party self-serving deals were done with local white elites and international capital. By 1996 Thabo Mbeki—then deputy president of South Africa, later successor to Nelson Mandela as leader of the ANC and president of South Africa—was calling himself a Thatcherite and the ANC had voluntarily imposed its own structural adjustment program on South Africa. Taxes on the rich were cut, exchange controls dropped, and tariffs protecting unionized South African workers from imports from sweat shops were abandoned. Around a hundred thousand jobs were lost each year and a million alone in 2001. Water, electricity, housing and health care were taken from those who couldn't pay.

The white elite was allowed to move its corporate assets to London and a small black elite made up of around 300 families became super rich. Unemployment reached 40 percent and by every measure (life expectancy, morbidity, access to food, water, etc.) the living conditions of the poor rapidly worsened. Heretical statistics, I know.

Scattered resistance to market fundamentalism was dealt with brutally. On May 16, 2000, Michael Makabane was shot dead at point-blank range during a peaceful protest against the exclusion of poor students from the University of Durban-Westville. That campus had been considered a hotbed of militant resistance to apartheid. While police repression had been brutal no students had ever been killed during the apartheid era. The local paper, now under black editorship, called for "tougher" action against protesting students (*Daily News*, May 17, 2000).

By 2002 over 6 million South Africans were HIV positive and without any access to the lifesaving medication that, even a not completely rabid neo-liberal budget, could safely satisfy. People were aghast at a comment made by the president's spokesperson that medicines that prevented mother-to-child transmission of the virus were undesirable because of the healthy orphans it left the state to deal with. The majority of the population are living on less than R140 (about $15) per month[1]. One in four black children do not have enough to eat every day. Only 3 percent of arable land had been redistributed and much of that had been given to black commercial farmers and not to landless peasants. Over a million people had been disconnected from water because they couldn't pay; 40,000 children were dying from diarrhea caused by dirty water each year. Cholera returned with a vengeance, infecting over 100,000 people in Kwa-Zulu Natal alone. People starved in rural areas, throngs of street-kids descended on every town to beg and prostitute themselves, petty-crimes soared, and the jails reached 170% capacity.

It was in these contradictory circumstances—with a government elected by the oppressed majority and using that power to carry out the program of big capital—that people began defending their homes from the private security companies hired to effect the state's eviction notices. Trade union and church leaders were speaking truth to power. Small groups were meeting in dingy offices bequeathed to the poor by white flight to gated suburbs, London and Sydney. They were discussing strategy, learning to say "Phansi ANC! Phansi!" (Down with the ANC! Down!) and planning meetings, strikes, and marches. Rivulets of humanity were back on the streets demanding land, a basic income grant, anti-AIDS medication, a halt to privatization, and dignity.

THE BETRAYAL of the South African liberation struggle has been documented by scholars like Dale McKinley, Hein Marais, Patrick Bond, and

John Saul.[2] Anyone who wants to hold on to the fantasies of South Africa as a liberated zone should read their books. The dirty deals have been recorded and the numbers are all there. This is a different kind of book. It aims to give some account of the lived experience of both the human cost of the ANC's capitulation to domestic and international capital and the growing resistance to the ANC. Especially, it hopes to express the conditions for the emergence of such a struggle and communicate the terms upon which it is taking place, for there is something special and encouraging at this level too.

You will meet in this book Sifiso Sithole. He is sixteen years old and from Soweto. He belongs to the Soweto Electricity Crisis Committee (SECC) that sponsors Operation Khanyisa ("To light up"). Sifiso is part of a hunted band of people who reconnect electricity to the homes of those who are too poor to pay the bills of the busy-being-privatized utility Eskom.

You will hear the story of Jasmine Samsodien. She lives at number 35 Heuningberg in Tafelsig, Cape Town. She turned to the Tafelsig Anti-Eviction Committee when police and council employees arrived to evict her in September 2001. Prevented from doing so by a mass uprising, the following month the council authorities cut her water and thereby a lifeline to her four children and three grandchildren. The inspirational response of the people of the Cape Flats is recorded in these pages.

Binisle Mzeku worked at Volkswagen South Africa in Uitenhage in the Eastern Cape for over a decade. At the beginning of 2000 he was one of 3,000 workers who went on strike against their own union. At issue was the sweetheart decision of National Union of Metalworkers of South Africa (NUMSA) to sign an agreement with management that eroded many shopfloor gains in the bloody battles of the 1980s.

At about the time Binisle heard from the Labour Appeal Court that he and over a thousand others had lost their jobs, Jane Smith was part of a union that participated in an illegal strike against the huge multinational, Engen, in Durban's South basin. The strike was about the casualization of labor, pollution and environmental degradation, and above all, as one worker put it, about dignity. It was a unique kind of strike as the whole community of Wentworth rose up to support the strikers whose own identity was transformed by the support they received.

In Chatsworth, Thulisile Christina Manqele lives in 173 Glenover Road, Block 92. Unemployed, desperately ill, with seven children to care for, her electricity and water were disconnected for non-payment. She turned to her neighbors in the Westcliff Flat Resident's Association. They turned for relief to the courts who had the job of interpreting the socioeconomic clauses in the supposedly "most progressive constitution in the world." The judges, though, found a clever way to look the other way and the community then took matters into their own hands. They have been illegally reconnecting water and fighting off the city council security men every time they have come to impose law and order since then.

Many of the different threads of struggle described in this book came together in August and September 2001, in massive protests against the South African government as it hosted the showpiece World Conference Against Racism, held in Durban. Community organizations came together and South Africa and the world had a new social movement to deal with, the Durban Social Forum. Although the book follows events no further, they have not come to a halt. The birth of a movement is described in this book. So much depends on it as we go into the future.

The response of the state to all these struggles has been uncompromising and brutal, ranging from vicious assaults, arrests, and the fabricating of charges and the labeling of activists as criminals. But paradoxically, the life of people in these communities has become increasingly sensuous. An active sense of community pervades. Spaces for living that are not bonded to the dollar sign have been carved open and are jealously protected while new ways of struggling that value human needs and desires are being imagined. These are fragile times and yet the scraggly kitten has already all the fierceness of a lynx.

All these community movements from Tafelsig in the Western Cape, to Soweto in Gauteng, and Chatsworth in Durban are signposts of something in South Africa. They are the force behind what has been called "South Africa's new revolution"—a revolution captured by Jon Jeter in these terms: "Seven years after voters of all races went to the polls for the first time, ending 46 years of apartheid and white rule, churches, labor unions, community activists and the poor in all-black townships are dusting off the protest machinery that was the engine of their liberation struggle. What most provokes South Africans' defiance today are what they see as injustices unleashed on this developing nation by the free-market economic policies of the popularly elected, black-led governing party, the African National Congress" (*Washington Post*, November 6, 2001).

The events narrated below reveal how struggle in the new South Africa may be rediscovered and re-created. But the story is not told in abstract terms. This is first and foremost an account from the frontlines of the establishment's undeclared war on the poor. It is, I am told, a heartening report because the war seems no longer to be one-sided.

1. The value of the South African currency, the rand, has fluctuated during the period dealt with in this book. Until 1984, the value of the rand was close to of the U.S. dollar. At the time the chain of events described in this book begins—that is, around mid-1999—the rand-dollar exchange rate was around R6/$. By the time of the World Conference Against Racism, in early September 2001, the rand was about R8.50/$. After September 11, 2001, the value of the rand fell sharply again, to a record low of R13.85/$.

2. E.g., Hein Marais, *South Africa: Limits to Change: The Political Economy of Transformation* (London: Zed Press, 1998); Patrick Bond, *Elite Transitions: From Apartheid to Neoliberalism in South Africa* (London: Pluto Press, 2000); John S. Saul, "Cry for the Beloved Country: The Post-Apartheid Denouement," *Monthly Review* 52:8 (January 2001), pp. 1–51.

1. fatima meer comes to chatsworth

Chatsworth came into being forty years ago with the passing of the Group Areas Act. It was laid out on either side of a ridge many kilometers long. There is a never-ending highway and railway line running the length of the ridge on its plateau. There are numberless roads leading down steep slopes on either side of the highway. Each of these side roads, in turn, are intersected by streets that run parallel to the highway so giving Chatsworth its sprawling, elongated feel and creating an urban space that is both like a maze and yet also a grid. Today it is home to 300,000 people—mostly, but by no means all, Indian.

If you were to sit in a compartment on the train to Chatsworth and look out of the window, you would see down each of these streets rows and rows of semi-detached two-story flats, painted in faded pastel shades of orange, blue, lilac, and pink. Atop each flat is a dark grey asbestos roof. The flats are so close together that it appears they too could be coaches waiting for an engine to draw them away. As the buildings blur by, you would see, every so often, a structure bigger than the rest; a school, a temple, a funeral parlor, a shop, a house belonging to a doctor or druglord.

At the very bottom of the ridge, where a valley is formed, the semi-detached flats mutate into huge, bulky tenement blocks containing six families a piece. Here the poorest of the people of Chatsworth have been put to live and die. These are the proverbial third-class coaches of the apartheid train: cramped, ugly, unsafe, and hidden from view.

In 1990 the Group Areas Act was repealed and liberation movements were unbanned. In 1994 the ANC came to power. Its leaders came to Chatsworth promising a better life for all. It appeared that a new engine had pulled into the station, promising to haul those living in the forgotten sidings of South Africa up onto the main line.

It seems natural that the hope of delivery from the state should have replaced struggle. The spears of opposition politics were beaten into the plowshares of policy. The RDP promised people-centered development. It would take some time, but gradually a better life would be attained for all.

But there was a dark side. Amidst the pageantry of change, there was a praetorian observance of the rules and values of the old. Shortly after elections, severe rent increases were promulgated. As the months passed, the shakedown became unremitting. As the new millennium approached, conditions in Chatsworth's flatlands were nasty, the authorities were brutish, and evidence of a better life in short supply. Echoes of the apartheid past were heard in the neo-liberal present. Evictions, relocation, and disconnections vied with promises of housing, water, and a culture of human rights. Community leaders were marked with the labels of agitator, radical, and counter-revolutionary, used interchangeably.

THIS WAS THE SITUATION encountered by Professor Fatima Meer when she arrived in Chatsworth at the beginning of May 1999. The internationally recognized sociologist, biographer of Nelson Mandela, patron of Jubilee 2000, and persecuted anti-apartheid activist led a small organization called the Concerned Citizens Group (CCG). Their mission, according to ads taken out in the local media, was to convince Indians not to vote for the "white parties" in the up-coming general elections; a reference to the National and Democratic parties, the parties that had survived from the "whites only" apartheid parliament. However, as the election campaign unfolded, the CCG's objective became one of garnering votes specifically for the ANC. The CCG's intervention was watched with interest by established political parties because the approximately 250,000 voters in this community could well determine which party won a majority in KwaZulu-Natal.

Meer and her merry band had crammed onto their letterhead the names of many among the Indian professional and business elite. Their analysis was that Indians were not voting for the ANC because of an inherently racist fear of Africans. Insinuated within this thinking was the view that the ANC was a party dedicated to uplifting the lives of the poor. A further assumption was that "Africans" alone were the poor. The role of Meer and the CCG was, borrowing from Leninist parlance, to bring revolutionary, non-racial consciousness from the outside to the masses who, on their own, could not move beyond a minority false consciousness.

The situation that confronted Meer was much more complex. There were a number of affluent Indians in Chatsworth. The local political hierarchy, in particular, had done well for themselves. But many of the flat dwellers who rented accommodation from the city council seemed impervious to her solicitations not to vote for white parties. They told her that they were "not concerned about their former oppressors but were angry at their present oppressors."[3] This they defined as the Durban Transitional Metropolitan Council, which was involved in water and electricity disconnections and evictions for non-payment of rates and rents. The residents took Meer from house to house showing her how many of them were unemployed, single mothers, or aged and infirm. They were patient with her, but a little hostile, for the council was dominated by the ANC—an organization Meer had served for over 50 years. Nowhere, she discovered, did representatives of this organization command the respect and admiration of decades before. Members of the CCG found the cool reception they received difficult to understand. Any political activist associated with the ANC, especially of Meer's generation, was accustomed to different throngs when visiting Chatsworth: respectful, not sullen; smiling, not going about their business resentful at the intrusion. Wasn't it the case that many of the ANC's leading officials today were once leaders of the civic associations of the 1980s that challenged apartheid-era city councils precisely on evictions and unaffordable rent increases? What had happened?

As is the way of sociologists, Meer decided to conduct a survey of the flat dwellers' socioeconomic circumstances. While this was still being planned, Winnie Mandela came to visit Chatsworth looking for votes. The tears she shed could well have summed up the interim results of the research. The statistics confirmed that something was terribly wrong. Meer expected evidence of some social and economic distress but the level of poverty and degradation was much worse than imagined. Unemployment was running at 70 percent, many children of school age were not in classrooms for lack of fees, diseases of poverty raged unchecked, and, when they were lucky, whole families were completely reliant on pensions and grants.

"It was difficult to imagine how people managed to feed themselves and their children, let alone pay rent or rates. Suddenly the thousands of rands in rental arrears that had been accumulated by residents made sense," was the comment of a CCG member after his first tour of Unit 3 or Bangladesh, as it is known. Contrary to government accusations, there was no "culture of non-payment." There was simply no income in these areas. What had taken root was an economics of non-payment.

Meanwhile, further storm clouds of distress were gathering. The clothing industry, traditional source of work for tens of thousands of people in Chatsworth, was in tatters. From a high of 435 employers in 1995, the industry now contained a paltry 166. The only other sources of income, grants and alms, also began decreasing. Countless mothers reported that their disability and child-care grants had been summarily stopped. Investigations showed that the state had begun making use of new criteria, designed to reduce costs, and was stripping its books of thousands of women whose children were older than seven. Begging, on the other hand, had become so widespread throughout the city that there was simply not enough traffic-light benevolence to go around.

Meer changed tack. In illhealth and against the admonishments of her doctors, she threw all her remaining energies into compiling a research report to present to the ANC government. Meer had made up her mind; if people were too poor to pay rates and rent through no fault of their own, then she'd be damned if her movement and government would throw them out onto the streets or cut off their lights and water. All she had to do was to show the ANC the proof.

In the process of gathering proof, she and other CCG members also spent time attending to the day-to-day problems of the community, learning anew about "material conditions." It was also a time of awakening for the various communities in whom hidden reserves of leadership suddenly became apparent. Individuals in the community drew confidence from the CCG's support in their grievance against this policeman or that "druglord." Some were willing to be elected onto Flat Resident associations and others to assist with the survey. As leadership in one area became more and more visible, so they inspired others. Members of the CCG, in turn, learned that their old categories of political thought were useless and developed new ones. While it still had a certain resonance, it was silly to even think of the area as "Indian." An increasing number of the flats were occupied by African tenants and, when the chips were down, everyone thought of themselves as a community, as "the poors." There was space for being black, but it was never certain what blackness was. At the same time it was ridiculous to talk of socialism and the working class. These were generally understood to be noble, but foreign, constructs. To attempt to hold anybody, a priori, to ideological principles proper to "the left" was neither possible nor desirable.

After she started her research, Professor Meer made no further calls on the Indian community to vote one way or the other. The elections came and went. She submitted her report to the ANC. After the elections, Meer was horrified that ANC councilors were among the most vociferous in insisting that electricity and water cut-offs and evictions be visited on the poor. Indeed, in one area, more than half the households were officially without electricity. While this was bad enough, councilors were now advocating water disconnections. Meer could not understand how, in the face of such obvious poverty, residents could be expected to come up with the approximately R400 a month the council required for rent, lights, and water. The disciples of a better life for all were behaving as if poverty itself was a crime.

Meer started asking questions. She demanded answers from ANC policy makers in local government. Some councilors tried to shout her down by insinuating she was standing up for Indian interests. Others talked about financial constraints to her face and about her advancing years behind her back. She persisted in the challenge. The rest is not yet history but the beginning of something historic: the struggle for the new South Africa. To understand this better, we should go back to the beginnings of the township of Chatsworth.

2. harinarian "moses" judhoo in the promised land

> Rooms have no doors and roofs have no ceilings. Walls are bag-washed with white lime. It is all rather typical of a horse stable.

—R.S. NAIDOO, *Daily News*, November 15, 1965.

AFTER THE PASSING of the Group Areas Act in 1950, thousands of Indians from all over Durban were corralled into Chatsworth's ten-square-kilometer precincts south of Durban. This "pernicious effort to segregate Indians en masse into special kraals, locations and townships" was a task the Durban City Council undertook with zeal.[1] This was not unexpected given Mayor Percy Osborne's boast in the 1950s that apartheid itself "was the traditional policy of the burgesses of Durban and their municipal representatives long before the Nationalists came to power." On a later occasion Osborne explained why he was such a fervent adherent of racial segregation: the Group Areas Act was "the lifeline whereby the European City of Durban will be saved."[2]

And so tens of thousands of Indians and as many Africans were forced to give up their lives in the areas they had called home and were packed off to the outer reaches of Durban. Whether by the shove of a baton or a bulldozer or simply bowing to the authority of the law, thousands of Indians suddenly found themselves on a sloped piece of land 25 kilometers from the city center. The township was initially to consist of nine self-contained units of tightly packed semi-detached flats ranged along the Higginson Highway. The tiny houses with whitewashed walls, roofs minus a ceiling, and a lone door led to an ironic refrain from residents that they came to the "promised land" (a reference to the apartheid state's promise of a better life in Chatsworth) and had found a stable.

It is worth pausing for a moment to record that the stables were themselves built on "stolen" land, formerly occupied by 600 Indian small farmers and a community of some 14,000. These families had farmed in the Cavendish, Welbedacht, and Zeekoei Valley areas from the turn of the twentieth century. The famous "Cavendish Bananas" were originally grown here. When land was needed for urbanized Indians displaced by apartheid, the apartheid government in perfect racial symmetry promptly seized such land from Indian farmers for a quarter of its price (*Natal Mercury*, October 13, 1960). Just as some residents were arriving to start a new life, others were coming to terms with the destruction of a lifetime's work.

HARINARIAN JUDHOO was one of those early residents. He came to a place he had vaguely heard referred to as "Chatsworth" in 1963. When he got there he pined after the network of friends and relatives he was forced to leave behind in Prospect Hall some 30 kilometers away. Sitting on a sandy hill, he looked at his wife Shakoon. Her stare was empty. She was exhausted from the two- hour walk from Clairwood. There was no transport to this godforsaken place. Shakoon seemed too tired to give attention to their sons, aged eleven and two, who took turns pulling on her sari. Harinarian thought of the two puppies he had left behind with a neighbor in Prospect Hall. The neighbors had decided to stay and fight.

For a time Harinarian contemplated holding on too. People delivered a pamphlet under his door that described the Group Areas Act as emanating from the most "depraved and inhumane forces of the land, for the most depraved and degrading act in our history—armed robbery in the name of the law." The newspaper was called *Fighting Talk*. But as the months passed there was a lot of talking but no collective action. He was finally convinced to move to Chatsworth when a city council official told him that there would be many jobs in nearby Mobeni. It was a chance to give his family a better life.

For the first year Harinarian could find no work. Shakoon grew more distant. All the time hundreds of people were arriving in Chatsworth. From Sea Cow Lake, Temple Halt, Riverside, Umhlanga, Berea, Sea View, Bellair, and Cato Manor they settled around him. But there was no family here. No one from whom to borrow a little, to tide the family over. Just strangers, pitched next to each other. Like on a gold rush. There were none of the monthly trips to the city center that had always lifted Shakoon's spirits.

After a year Harinarian found a job. At first he did not tell his wife. Every morning he got up early and went to the shoe-making factory. Only at the end of the second week when he received his brown packet containing four rand did he tell her. A year later Leela was born. A daughter. How he had craved a girl. He wanted her to have everything. He walked to work to save money to buy her little nice things. He worked overtime, he worked weekends. Shakoon, too, grew visibly younger. How many nights had she gone without, he wondered, so that he and the children could eat?

After three years of non-stop work Harinarian was getting more and more tired. He pushed on with the same punishing hours. There was no time for temple. No time for Leela. The fumes on the factory floor made him cough incessantly. His fingers showed the sharp pinpricks of the sewing needle as his eyesight declined. One day the body would not get up. The next day he was fired. He was in his mid-forties. It was 1967. He had kept up-to-date with payments for rent. He owed nobody.

The cough became more insistent. He could not hide the blood on the handkerchief from Shakoon. Unlike the last time of unemployment she cared for him. She gave him attention. But strangely it was Leela's attention Harinarian craved. When he had come home at the end of the working week, Leela had clung to him as he slowly conjured goodies from his pockets. But she soon tired of the game after a few months of unemployment. Was it his imagination or was there no magic anymore?

Harinarian was starting to lose control over his youngest boy, Dharam. Dharam was forced to go to school after lunch because of the shortage of schools. He was one of some 30,000 kids who were part of the platoon system. But he had taken to hanging about the streets in the morning, joining a number of unsupervised kids, and then complaining of being tired in the afternoon when it was time to go to school.

A little light was spread by Ram, the oldest boy, who finished school. The Springfield Training College was prepared to take him. But he would need to take two buses. Ram, without asking, got up everyday as his father had once done and went to find work. The bills were mounting. The rent and electricity account averaged R18 a month. The council kept warning him that he would be evicted. Shakoon, with five-year-old Leela in tow, took to looking for a job. This woman, who agonized over marrying one rung below her caste, now stood on the doorsteps of the lowest castes asking to wash their clothes. How class can turn caste upside down.

On April 17, 1969, the Judhoo family were thrown out. Ram had found a low paying job in a furniture factory in Merebank. But it was never going to be enough to keep his house in Road 734. The arrears had climbed to R146.

When the reporters arrived they found Harinarian on a pavement surrounded by the family possessions. He held onto a pet tortoise. This was the second week they had lived outside the sealed house. Everyday Shakoon set out to town to find cheaper accommodation. In the third week they secured a room in a corrugated iron shack in Welbedacht. A temporary arrangement.

The readers of the *Daily News* were moved by the plight of the Judhoo family. The newspaper reported (May 14, 1969) that readers had donated R53. A group of businessmen promised to make up the shortfall. But Harinarian knew it was over. He would fall behind again. Ram would never be a teacher. Leela would never cling to him again. He had failed Shakoon. One day she came back with an odd smile on her face and told him they had been saved. Saved by the Jehovah's Witnesses. Shakoon was now "Mary." The worse their suffering became the more she glowed, as if she was getting closer to God.

What did he tell people who asked after him? About his dreams of a better life. How hard he worked. The family he left behind in Prospect Hall and never saw again. The newspaper that referred to the Group Areas Act as armed robbery. The humiliation of not being able to take care of his innocent, neglected daughter.

1   P.S. Joshi, *The Struggle for Equality* (Bombay: Hind Kitabs, 1951), p. 258
2   B. Maharaj, "Apartheid, Urban Segregation and the Local State: Durban and the Group Areas Act in South Africa," *Urban Geography* 18, pp. 135–54.

3. how are these people
even able to exist?

> He took a note from his pocket. It stated: "You, Venkatsamy,
> are notified by the City Council to leave your plot number so and so"
> . . . He said, "Ma, I've been living in this place for the last
> fifty years. Where do I go now?" When I went back
> a few weeks later, the old man had died. It was the death
> of one who did not want to live anymore.

—DR. K. GOONAM, quoted in G. Vahed, *The Making of Indian
Identity in Durban 1914–49.*

IN 1964, an economist visiting Chatsworth said he was amazed at "how some of these people are even able to exist" (*Daily News*, September 10, 1964). In her 1967 presidential address to the Durban Indian Benevolent Society, Dr. Khorshed Ginwala spoke of the "sordid existence" that is Chatsworth: "Indian employees of the municipality, who belong to the laboring class, earn a maximum wage of R36 per month. It costs R49 a month to keep a family at Chatsworth which is about twelve miles away from the city center. Rent, electricity and transport costs alone total R17.72. Groceries cost R18.20; bread and butter R4.80; vegetables R8.28. No money is available for meat, clothing and laundry and as it is this exceeds by R8.13 the wage of R36." She posed the obvious, but still haunting question: "Without begging, stealing or borrowing, what avenues are available to men and women to supplement this amount?" (*Daily News*, November 4, 1967).

Particularly hard hit were the people whose expenses, after forced removal, quadrupled overnight. This was the case of the Magazine Barracks residents, forcibly removed from central Durban and housed in the sub-economic flat complexes in Chatsworth. Although living in atrocious conditions, in Magazine Barracks, the 7,000 people resisted the move to Chatsworth. In 1964 the rent at the barracks was 87 cents for a two room flat inclusive of electricity and water compared to between R2 and R10 per month in Chatsworth.[1] Once relocated, people would also have the added burden of transport costs. By being relocated they would be cut off from the myriad of casual jobs that the proximity of the harbor and golf courses provided.16

These realities did stop the council from putting up the rent of sub-economic rental stock in 1967 ranging from 10 to 20 percent. Residents were informed of this in a circular put out by the city treasurer, O.D. Gorven. Community structures sprung up and Chatsworth residents started to mobilize and set up a shadow town council. People divided themselves into wards and elected committees. This led to a great deal of consternation in City Hall as the community was raising the specter of dual power. Over a thousand people attended a mass meeting, braving the attentions of the Special Branch—the police agency responsible for political surveillance—who closely monitored proceedings. Council member George Naidoo pointed to the fact that the houses were "jerry-built" and liable to become slums in a few years. Naidoo also criticized wealthy Indians: "I have lost respect for the leaders of the Indian community. They are happy in their R50,000 Isipingo and Reservoir Hills homes and they completely ignore the needs of the people who keep them there." The representative of Ward 3 brought the house down when he referred to Chatsworth as a "mushroom town with no character. It resembles the tenement houses of the time of King Henry VIII." He spoke as if from personal experience. Besides condemning the increase, the committee also resolved to seek legal opinion on the council's ultimatum to tenants to "Pay up or hand in your keys" (*Sunday Tribune*, September 3, 1967; *Daily News*, September 4, 1967).

The council adopted a twofold approach to the mobilization. It castigated the leaders as revolutionaries who were inciting the poor. At the same time it continued with evictions, creating fear, and fostering division. The Durban city council treasurer reported that in 1967, 411 people were in arrears and thirty families were evicted during the months of September, October, and November. In a press statement he said, "It is the council's policy at all times to endeavor to assist tenants, although it will be appreciated that the council cannot suffer rental losses by allowing tenants to remain in occupation when rentals are unpaid" (*Daily News*, February 3, 1968).

One could not escape the impression, reading newspaper reports of the time, that through the years, Council simply operated as an efficient debt collector. In 1968, amidst the obvious poverty of residents, the city treasurer could report a surplus of R48,260 (*Daily News*, December 10, 1968).

The council was able to strike fear in the hearts of tenants by mechanically implementing its policies, totally without regard to circumstance. This was intended to instill a culture of payment. But treating people as numbers, like the numbers that served as road names, increasingly spurred resistance. On February 11, 1969, the *Natal Mercury* reported that, according to Durban city council policy, members of a family occupying a council home in Chatsworth would have to vacate the house after the death of a father and mother. This meant that children in Chatsworth not only became orphans on the death of their parents, but they also became homeless. An official of the city treasurer's department was quoted as saying that they were forced to take these steps "because of the terrible shortage of houses for Indians." The logic seemed to be that the shortage of houses was to be dealt with by evicting one set of persons and putting others in their place. Eventually the council conceded there was a housing shortage. But when people tried to make do they were harshly dealt with. In February 1974, a widow was evicted from her house in Road 516 because she had shared her council house with her married daughter and a relative. The widow, Mrs. Muthalamma Chetty, and her four young children were forced to live in the open veld. After the issue received media coverage, the deputy city treasurer, Gordon Haygarth, apparently moved by the plight of the children eating and sleeping in the open, gave her a reprieve on compassionate grounds (*Natal Mercury*, February 16, 1974).

The council responded to anti-poverty protests by continuing with increases, accompanied with a "no nonsense approach." In December 1974 it sent out a notice to tenants in Crossmoor in Unit 11 asking tenants to pay higher rentals or vacate their homes by January 1975. The notice read: "If, however, you feel that you are unable to meet the higher rental, this letter must be regarded as formal notice of termination of your lease with effect from January 3. In this event kindly hand in keys to the dwelling to that office." The Crossmoor Civic Association protested, but to no avail.

One of the problems for the more well-to-do Indians was that the Group Areas Act forced them in many instances to remain in Chatsworth. It would be wrong to say that they developed any race or class solidarity because of their confinement. As early as 1969 the chairman of the Southern Durban Indian Local Affairs Committee (LAC), J.N. Reddy, speaking on behalf of richer Indians in Chatsworth, urged the city council not to mix cheap sub-economic houses with expensive dwellings as this would alter the character of the area. The LAC was reacting to a call by the Indian Child

Welfare Society that houses for low- and high-income groups be mixed so that the "upper-class Indians can uplift the lower-class people" (*Natal Mercury*, April 9, 1969). Later that year he was to also support rent increases in the area arguing that it could easily be seen "that the sub-economic rents are not so bad after all." This was despite the Chatsworth Civic Association demonstrating that "tenants are forced to pay 20 percent or more of their earnings in rentals" (*Daily News*, October 31, 1969).

Certain areas of Chatsworth then became the preserve of the middle class. Mobeni, for example, was strategically placed at the entrance to Chatsworth. Silverglen was placed between Units 2 and 3. Kharwastan and Umhlatuzana were good addresses adjacent to Unit 10. These pockets of affluence served as a cover for the socioeconomic degeneration that was enveloping the areas where the council had accommodation for rent. It also created difficulties for a unified response as, in a manner typical of Indian and generally anti-apartheid politics, it was the well-to-do who framed the issues and had access to the media and the existing political organizations. Interestingly even "progressive" organizations sidelined issues of poverty and lack of housing, which received attention disproportionate to the scale of the suffering in Chatsworth at the time.

AMONG THE FIRST RESIDENTS of Chatsworth were shack dwellers from the Amanzimnyama area of Clairwood. Indians had settled in the area from the 1920s and had access to market gardens adjacent to the settlement. Within 21 months the community was destroyed and many forced into Chatsworth. One of the first to move was Mr. Anamuthoo who was employed at Consolidated Textile Mills as a spinner for over two decades. He had lived in shack A90 in Clairwood for 22 years. He moved into house 290, Road 328 on September 30, 1963. The records show that when asked the reason for his application to move from Clairwood to Chatsworth, Anamuthoo's response was, "We must apply."[2]

Intrigued by the simplicity of Mr. Anamuthoo's comment, I attempted to track him down 36 years later. I arrived at the residence of Ramiah Anamuthoo but he had passed away on November 29, 1976. His wife Ankamma still lived in the flat. She was 81 years old. Her son, Antony, one of eight children, joined us. He lived in a flat around the corner. He was 14 when they arrived in Unit 3. The family lived at 262 Whitehall Place, Jacobs. Before moving to Whitehall Place they had a five-bedroom house in Balfour Road but it was destroyed during the 1949 Indo-African riots.

Slowly Ankamma, without frills, told me her story. They were first offered a house in Unit 1 but they did not qualify as Ramiah was not earning enough. By the time they moved, Ramiah had already worked at Consolidated Textile Mills for 27 years. After 31 years of service, Ramiah's take-home pay was R8 a week. Gross annual remuneration, according to his 1968 income tax return, was R459.47. In Clairwood, Ramiah Anamuthoo supplemented the family income by going fishing to the "Wests." With the long distances from Chatsworth to the sea, this was only occasionally possible. Ankamma also worked at the Natal Bottle Exchange for 11 years and then Bailes for 11 years. Ankamma gets a pension of R520. Most of it goes for rent, lights, and water, which come to between R345 and R360. She has bought goods at Shaik Supply Store for the last thirty years on a monthly credit system. She is up to date with her rent. However she moans about the escalating costs. She shows me a rent slip for R28.46 from 1978. Another from 1982, R 37.98. Now R350.

Their son Antony has eight children, one of them from a previous marriage. His first marriage broke up because his in-laws felt he was spending too much money on his father's funeral. At the age of 15, Antony went to work. He worked at R. Faulks footwear for 15 years starting with the princely salary of 60 cents a week. After a period of unemployment in the 1980s, he found work at Delano Footwear in Unit 10 Chatsworth. He was put on indefinite short- time. He has not worked since 1997 and has pawned both his and his wife's sewing machines to get money for food. He believes that the shoe industry has collapsed because of "cheap imports from China." Unable to meet the rent and provide for his family he has built a structure in his mother's back garden to try to do some sewing. But he needs money to get his sewing machine back. His son in Standard 8 seeks refuge at the grandmother's.

Antony still hopes to get back into the footwear industry, but the odds are against that. Cheap imports have escalated in the last decade rising from 12.86 million pairs in 1989 to 50.83 million in 1996. A 1997 South African Clothing Textile and Workers Union (SACTWU) secretariat report indicated that since 1990 13,000 jobs have been lost in the footwear and leather industries. At the same time production has declined from 72.6 million pairs in 1990 to 48.3 million pairs in 1997.[3]

I look at Antony and know that at 49 years of age he will never work again. He left school at 15 to help his family as the cost of living in Chatsworth escalated. He has been put on indefinite short-time as a result of government tariff-lowering policies which have destroyed the shoe indus-try. Will his kid in Standard 8, sharing a house with seven other people and aware of his family's plight, have any reason to hope for a better life?

But it is Ankamma's hurt that I feel. She is always so neatly clad in staid saris. Her house is immaculate. She keeps returning to the theme of why 70 percent of her pension is gobbled up by rent and electricity and water. One can sense she is worried about Antony. My last image of Ankamma is of her unfolding her husband's certificate of 25 years' service received in 1962.

1   Bill Freund, "The Destruction of Communities, 1930–1980: The Indian Working Class of Durban and the Group Areas Act," paper presented to African Studies Institute, University of Witwatersrand, 1993.

2   Quoted in D. Scott, "Communal Space Construction: The Rise and Fall of Clairwood and District," Ph.D. dissertation, University of Natal, Durban, 1994, p. 357.

3   H. Deedat et al, *Research into the Effects of Globalization on the Leather and Footwear Sectors in South Africa* (Cape Town: ILRIG, 2000).

4. *a social time bomb starts ticking*

The authorities have done little to develop the area.
No community hall, no play lots, no parks: and yet the white
planned townships have all these amenities.

—S. GOVENDER, Social Worker, *Daily News*, August 27, 1968

I agree there is a need for amenities. But can you live in amenities?

—VEDA THOMPSON, Chair of the Durban City Council's
Housing Committee, *Sunday Tribune*, September 1, 1968

MANY OF THE RESIDENTS of Chatsworth had come from areas where they had developed a number of social organizations that created a sense of community in a hostile and discriminatory political environment. Geographer Diane Scott has written powerfully of the nurturing of communal bonds in Clairwood based on ties of trust, friendship, sociability, obligation, and mutual support overlaid with a framework of kinship and religious norms. Over decades "temples, schools, halls, clinics, and cemeteries became landmarks in Clairwood and District and symbols of communal sacrifice and solidarity."[1]

With relocation, thousands poured into Chatsworth and set up home alongside people they did not know. Families were broken up as the housing scheme only allowed for nuclear families. This was unlike the areas the residents came from where families paid for one rental site, "shared a common pot, household goods and even clothing." This created additional financial burdens as families had to meet separate rental payments and had to finance "a considerable amount of duplication of possessions."[2]

From the outset, rents were at least four times higher in Chatsworth than in Clairwood. Repayments were calculated on the basis of 25 percent of salaries while the average rental paid by Indians in Durban constituted 13 percent of their household incomes. Scott makes the point that the creation of a segregated city had the effect of locking "black moderate income earners into a system of credit and direct long-term dependence on wage earning and the state as opposed to their relatively higher levels of independence as occupiers of informal space."[3] This was still the period of the economic boom though, where unemployment was less than 20 percent. It was when the economy started to contract and credit escalate that this dependence started to rebound on the state.

The houses themselves provided a far from cozy sanctuary. The hollow cement walls inevitably cracked under the slightest pressure, the door frames almost immediately fell apart and the absence of interior doors meant that privacy was nonexistent. Built on steep slopes and with narrow staircases to the top floor the houses became a prison for the aged. More and more youngsters escaped the home for the privacy of the street. And with this development came a proliferation of street gangs.

In the absence of social and cultural venues and the broader networks of their previous abodes, alcohol abuse increased. Suicide and divorce rates spiraled upwards. In a detailed report on 31 families carried out in 1976, the University of Durban-Westville's Department of Social Work found that alcoholism existed in 10 families, 18 experienced severe marital discord while 11 instances of child neglect were recorded.[4] A survey to determine the need for a creche in Unit 3 found that nearly 60 percent of preschool children were left to their own devices or looked after by other kids. Some 64 percent of the school-going youngsters were left on their own in the afternoons. One mother took to locking up her five children (the oldest was nine years old) when she went to work each morning.

This situation was exacerbated by the long distances that people travel to work. Researchers found that over 90 percent of Chatsworth workers were away from work for over 10 to 11 hours every workday. Many left home at 4:30 A.M. and got back after 6:30 P.M. Some 70 percent spent at least an hour each way commuting, roughly equal to an extra day's productive work a week.[5] The advent of the railway line proved a failure while the struggle for a second access road succumbed to the racism of the Stainbank family who donated a piece of land to nature conservation that the second road would need to traverse. The donations were given in piecemeal fashion so as to make "any alternative route near the reserve an impossibility" (*Post*, May 7, 1986). John Stainbank would not allow cars driven by nonwhites to travel "through a residentially proclaimed white district which he says is not only objectionable but against government policy" (*Natal*

Mercury, June 3, 1992). Indeed the council had maintained that "one race should not travel through the residential areas of another."[6]

The breakdown of the patriarchal extended family, the increase in single mothers and the loosening from the conservative bonds of religious organization characterizing their previous environment did create the possibilities for a less oppressive lifestyle. But this was not the focus of the political activists of the time. In fact, many were linked to patriarchal religious organizations that saw traditional family hierarchies as the only form of family.

All the while, the council vigorously enforced its policies that held that "segregation demands effective boundaries. . . . The boundaries must in fact be barriers." As is so often the case, the violence of the system turned inwards. Alcoholism, suicide, child abuse, and gangsterism escalated.

FROM THE MID-1970S gangsterism thrived. This coincided with the arrival of Mandrax on the illicit drug market. Bag ladies brought in the drugs from India. Some of the bag ladies were afforded near mythological status, like Mother India from Unit 5. Her daughter remains incarcerated in a Mumbai prison for procuring Mandrax.

"Buttons," the street name for Mandrax, came to replace dagga as the drug of choice. With it came a more lucrative market and violent territorial battles ensued. Gruesome murders became commonplace. In the early 1980s, schoolchildren at Crossmoor Secondary came across human flesh in the school tennis court. It turned out to be the body of Tokaieye Farouk, a local gangster who had been murdered. His body had been chopped into small pieces. Then there was the call box murder. A woman was violently assaulted and stuffed in a call box. The killer was "an addict" from the area. Chatsworth was getting used to blood. The weapons were limited to knives and bush-knives though.

Style was terribly important. The Long Coat Boys (LCBs) spent hours grooming themselves. They all wore long leather jackets that had to be manufactured by a company called Pointer or Vella. Weekends saw many gangsters immaculately attired in three-piece suits, Crockett and Jones shoes, topped with ten-gallon hats. After a while, the dandies, who were still somewhat integrated into the community, gave way to more hard-core gangs like the Dirty Dozen and the Drain Rats. They spent less time in front of the mirror and more time on the streetcorner. Gang related graffiti was a common sight on the walls across the township. Gangsters were known for their big American cars. Preeminent were KY and Bra who used to prowl around Unit 11 in a big American V8 called "Ladies Eyes." KY is still alive serving a second 30-year sentence for murder.

Shebeens also served as a lucrative source of income. Fowl Auntie's shebeen in Unit 2 was a meeting place and still operates today. Gaveen Krish's, in Unit 3, sold a concoction of pineapple, potato, and brown bread that was boiled and then allowed to steam.

The gambling game, call-card, became a major social event. It was also very lucrative for the "box man" who provided the cards and security and was entitled to 10 percent of the bets cast. Soon each unit had one "big man" who controlled the card games, the shebeen, and the drug traffic. Mainly feared, the big man sometimes also played the role of popular hero, whose feats of bravery were related secondhand at bus stops and in school yards.

The youth, during this period, were immersed in the city matinee set. Clubs in the city center, like Dallas, Modules, and Fun City, located in the legendary Butterworth Hotel, were the popular hangouts. There were no clubs in Chatsworth and the matinee allowed the youth access to transport back home. The matinees were linked to the bus culture. Big sound, curtains, and speed made the buses special. Many a courtship began on these adrenalin-laden trips to town, away from the parental gaze. Children would do anything to get enough money for Saturday's fare. With that also came the fight for control. "Rank" Bala was a notorious figure who controlled the Unit 7 bus rank. Until he was murdered in the early 1980s, in a confrontation with the local community, no one dared question his decision to allow a bus to operate or not.

The early 1980s was the wildest period in Chatsworth's history. This was partly a function of the lack of police resources. For a long time the whole of Chatsworth was served by a small police station in Unit 2 with access to a couple of vehicles. It is no coincidence that it was precisely during this time that the South African economy was lurching into crisis. Unemployment began to escalate while policing, though upgraded, concentrated on the political threat with a blind eye being cast to "social excesses." Indeed, many of the drug lords were linked to the local police who were linked to the security apparatus. Often the community found it hard to tell the difference between the gangsters and the police. The most notorious of the police units was the "A team" who were, themselves, repeatedly brought up on assault and murder charges. The "rogue element" in the police force was to consolidate its position in the new police station in Unit 5. It did not come as a shock to many Chatsworth residents that some members of the Chatsworth police force were implicated in a R31 million armed robbery. By the mid-1990s, gangsters were a pale shadow of their former selves. This was mainly brought about by their breaking the golden rule of drug dealing: never start using your own product.

1   Diane Scott, "Communal Space Construction: The Rise and Fall of Clairwood and District" (unpublished Ph.D. dissertation, University of Natal, Durban, 1994), p. 365.
2   G.M. Maasdorp and N. Pillay, *Urban Relocation and Racial Segregation* (Durban: Dept. of Economics, University of Natal, 1977), p. 133.
3   Scott, "Communal Space Construction," p. 349.
4   G.C. Oosthuizen and J.H. Hofmeyr, *Socio-Religious Survey of Chatsworth* (Durban: Institute of Social and Economic Research, 1981), p. 18.
5   P. Corbett, *Housing Conditions at Chatsworth* (Durban: Institute for Social and Economic Research, 1980).
6   B. Maharaj and S. Govender, "Segregation, Buffer Zones and Transport Routes: A Case Study of the Second Access Road to Chatsworth"(unpublished paper).

5. the struggle and its fruits: from the militant eighties to the end of apartheid

IN 1980 AN INVESTIGATION by the Chatsworth Indian Child and Welfare Society found that mass unemployment, runaway fathers of "illegitimate" babies, and an increasing divorce rate were accelerating the number of Chatsworth residents relying on state grants to find their next meal. The investigation found that one in every eight families living in the area relied on some kind of grant. Some families were resorting to adopting children as a means of income as the Department of Indian Affairs paid foster parents R42 per month for every child they adopted.

The newly inaugurated Chatsworth Housing Action Committee (CHAC) began to galvanize larger and larger protests. They opposed the council's attempt to force the sale of the houses upon the residents. Their argument was based on the fact that because the residents had been forced to pay increasing rentals over the years, aside from transport costs to get to work, houses had been paid for many times over. It was ridiculous that the council now demanded R4,500 for the houses. The residents' legal representative, Mr. Mike Govindsamy, added that the flats were of poor quality and had barely managed to remain standing for 15 years—the lifespan of the houses was not expected to exceed 20 years. He also added that it needed to be taken into account that residents were victims of forced removals and were given no choice of their place of abode (*Sunday Tribune*, October 26, 1980).

The council remained intransigent to the protests against rent increases and the sale of houses. Councilor Neil MacLennan held that the issue was "not whether the people are poor, but whether the rents are reasonable and rational" (*Sunday Tribune*, March 2, 1980).

Evictions continued apace. In July 1982, Mrs. Daisy Rani Pillay was evicted from her home in Road 240 House 495 for being R160 in arrears. The

35

only financial support that Mrs Pillay, her two children, her 55- year-old mother, and disabled brother received was a R60 grant for the children. Her monthly rental was R60. In addition, Rani was in the final month of her pregnancy. Perhaps Councilor Steyn mistook that for being well fed. While pleading her case at the city treasurer's department, she heard from an official that her furniture had already been removed. After the media highlighted the case, she was given a reprieve of a few days. A city official, John Muir, warned that "we have since given the family a temporary reprieve and they have made arrangements to pay R55 a month." However, he was quick to add that "if they do not pay this amount at the end of the month, they will be evicted again" (Post, July 28, 1982).

Responding to increased anti-apartheid mobilization after the 1980 school boycotts, the state instituted a host of reforms in 1983. With regard to Indians and coloreds it proposed representation in a tricameral parliamentary system. Hoping to win legitimacy for the system and form a black buffer against African aspirations, it was sensitive enough not to do anything to spur on extra-parliamentary forces. There was a noticeable cut back in evictions, limited mainly to those accused of "unseemly behavior." The tricameral parliament did attract people like Rajbansi and J.N. Reddy from Chatsworth, but with only a tiny percentage of people voting for them. On the other side of the divide "Indian" politicians and professional middle-class people assumed prominence in the national movement for liberation. The Natal Indian Congress (NIC) played a major role in the United Democratic Front (UDF) and in the Durban Housing Action Committee (DHAC). However, the NIC was never able to build a mass base in Chatsworth, thriving instead on concluding pacts with the leadership of other "groups" and remaining somewhat aloof from the community's economic, as opposed to political, predicament.

Local civic organizations started to assert themselves instead. Protests in Chatsworth became more frequent and a clear set of demands started to emerge. In one such protest in July 1989, 300 protesters converged on the Regional Offices of the House of Delegates. They were tear gassed and two people were arrested. Sharm Maharaj, secretary of the DHAC, arrived on the scene to tell the media that the demand was for more affordable rents (Natal Mercury, July 6, 1989). During this season of marches, boycotts, and rallies from every conceivable quarter, as students, workers, churches, civic associations, and other groups all came out in support of each other's demands, the DHAC grew in strength. It was a year before the National

Party would be forced to abandon apartheid as revolt in South African cities intensified.

The DHAC organized protests across the city under the slogan that apartheid had made housing artificially unaffordable. Their demand was for more affordable housing. Their paid spokesperson was an ambitious forty-something activist who seldom smiled and spoke somewhat abrasively in clipped tones. His name was Trevor Bonhomme. He had marked himself for bigger things.

THERE WERE GREAT EXPECTATIONS that the birth of a non-racial democracy would put an end to evictions and forced removals and usher in a new, more people-centered government. In July 1994, eviction notices were served on 950 tenants who were in arrears. Water and electricity cut offs followed, as well as an increase in electricity charges together with fore-warnings of further increases. The general talk in the township was that these were to be understood as the last acts of vindictive white officials.

In May 1995, the city council's new housing director and former DHAC activist, Vidu Vedalankar, called for an increase in rentals in the Greater Chatsworth area. Although hope was still the dominant emotion with which the people of Chatsworth received their government, an element of dismay and even anger began to be displayed in the township. People questioned the call for rent increases on the basis that DHAC—where the local government leaders, now enforcing the increases, had got their start in politics—had argued that they were struggling for more affordable rents and that the previous city council had created artificially high rents. Slogans may change, but not facts. Vedalankar, or anyone else who was in power on the strength of promises of mass housing delivery, had not explained how these facts had changed, or come out into the open to admit that they were now comfortable with the inequity of throwing people out of their homes.

These pronouncements coincided with similar anti-poor policy formulation on a number of other fronts. But when attempts were made to engage former comrades on these issues, they were always busy, distant, and somehow disapproving. Hope still sprang eternal and so this uncertain situation inspired no protests. The government had always issued strange and hard- hearted diktats from on high. Surely these comrades would not act. This was a time when 40 percent of all tenants were in arrears (*Daily News*, May 12, 1995). They knew that. Unemployment was on the increase and conditions being what they were, it was inevitable that more and more people would fall into arrears. These instincts were partly correct. So soon after parliamentary democracy was ushered in, there would be no iron fist from a new government.

It took the City Council two years of democracy before they called upon the chief constable, once again, to fetch the police dogs from the kennels and reach for the tear-gas canisters in the Old Fort Road armory. In May 1996, a detachment of 50 security personnel rolled into Unit 3 in Chatsworth in four-wheel-drive pickups and began disconnecting water and electricity, throwing furniture and other belongings onto the street, before sealing doors of flats that were suddenly empty.

It is impossible to chronicle how disillusionment turned into dismay and finally antagonism. At first, people say they felt utterly alone and leaderless. Some spectators tried to resist but were easily driven off by police. Others discussed the evictions wherever they could, trying to provoke in others the outrage they felt. Bus stops and washing taps became centers of lamentation for weeks after the first evictions. Many wondered when it would happen to them. The people targeted in the first round of police action seemed to be random examples. Some owed relatively little.

Church leaders were reluctant to come forward and confront the evictions. Individuals rushed around looking for cash. Heirlooms worth R50 were pawned for half their worth as were portable television sets and fishing rods. In at least two cases, the young daughters of the family began contributing to the family finances through prostitution. But it was not enough. The majority of people had nothing more to sell. There were no jobs; only crime and the lottery offered any hope.

The first few evictions were not immediately followed up. It is not entirely clear why this was so. Informants in local government suggest that, however puny the resistance encountered, councilors were still too new at the job to order blood to be spilt. Others say that the squeeze from the national government on the local sphere's budget was not yet being felt. The 1996 eviction was a trial run ordered by those in the ANC who were quickest to be converted to neo- liberal economics. But the experiment was called off, lest it interfere with preparations for the first round of municipal elections. The people relaxed and rationalized. Struggle plumbers and electricians illegally reconnected supplies and life went on. Residents say that the first round of 1996 evictions seemed a "mistake," a brief and violent performance by an essentially benevolent but remote power.

Nevertheless disillusionment and dismay had set in. City council officials were regarded by many as "sell-outs" and "fat-cats" that had abandoned the township to pursue their own interests in the city. It was a sporadic and uneven process characterized by national "news" events which breathed new life into the Rainbow Nation and local experiences that called this optical illusion into question. For 24 months thereafter, a victory for the national soccer team, affectionately named "Bafana Bafana," would vie with a flurry of two-page eviction notices for attention in the mind of citizens in Chatsworth—as would parliamentary ceremonies vie with a new rash of retrenchments resulting from the signing of a trade deal.

By 1998 experience won out. Local government elections were over. The eviction letters were now delivered by the sheriff of the court. Something official was afoot. In response, new leaders were starting to emerge and there was militant talk against evictions. Suddenly, as in 1996, force was again used to effect evictions. In a bloody confrontation in Unit 3, residents fought running battles with armed city council security personnel. A pregnant woman was tear- gassed. She subsequently gave birth to a deformed baby. Saras Chetty, who was injured in the fracas, died two weeks later. In a spontaneous and inexplicably well-attended protest, over 2,000 Chatsworth residents, ferried to town in some 60 buses and 50 taxis, protested at the Durban city hall. Hassan Rehmane, from the Bayview Flat Dwellers Action Committee, launched during the 1988 evictions, had this to say at the time: "We are not asking for handouts. How are people who have not had jobs for three or four years expected to pay debts, which in some cases are as much as R20,000 and rising every month. Our demand to scrap arrears are aimed to give people a fresh start, a chance to better themselves" (*Post*, August 12, 1998). Such a huge show of strength in the city center had the desired effect. For the time being, evictions were called off.

There was no organization to absorb and direct the militancy. Many were so terrified that they went without food to keep up with payments. There were also socially regressive responses to the attack launched on residents. The social fabric, thin as it was, started tearing. Men resented the role played by "their women." Drug taking and violence were rampant. Radha Samuel came home one day in 1998 to find her husband's naked body perched over a cupboard. He had been killed by gangsters in another area and his corpse brought in through the back window. A cigarette was stuck in his mouth. Radha buried him. She paid her rent by washing clothes in Unit 3. Weathered from the backbreaking work, she was up-to-date with her payments. But she had to give up many essentials. She expects she will soon fall behind as people do not have money to pay for the washing of clothes anymore.

There were others whose lives were so decrepit that there was no longer any fighting back. Ms. Happiness Shinga, also from Unit 3, had her water and lights cut off and faced eviction. She and her husband had moved from the shacklands of Umlazi to start a new life. She was raped near the Higginson Highway and was subsequently found to be HIV positive. Her husband committed suicide when she told him. She survives on handouts from the neighbors and the local church. When I met her she was lying in bed waiting to die. Her electricity had been cut and she was facing eviction. Her young children hovered in the background. The oldest, Faith, just 11, wrapped herself around a plastic shower curtain that served as a door. She faced demons of her own. She too, by a separate rape, was HIV positive. Council officials were adamant that Ms. Shinga could only stay if she paid her rent regularly and undertook to pay the outstanding amount.

Ms. Shinga's case was dealt with in the same way as Ms. Neelawa Singh's in 1978. Ms. Singh and her three children (one of them a nine-month-old baby) were evicted from their Road 1021 flat. She had been retrenched from her job two months earlier and her husband had not paid maintenance for ten months. She had to sleep on the stairs of the block of flats while her furniture lay on the roadside. A council spokesperson said they had stayed the eviction for a month. However, they could not stay this indefinitely. "Eviction is our last step, we do not like doing it, it is only our last resort. We are prepared to accept about R50 from Ms. Singh now, and we will let her back into the flat, on condition she pays back the outstanding amount regularly every month" (*Post*, September 13, 1978). Twenty years on, despite this "miracle" of democracy, one cannot but help matching these platitudes with those of Mr. Yunus Sacoor, the manager of Metro Council's Formal Housing Division, who wrote, in February 2000, that "the Council does not look forward to evicting people, but does so only in the last resort" (*Natal Mercury*, February 17, 2000).

b. "we are the poors"

We are not Indians, we are the poors.

—GIRLIE AMOD, Chatsworth, October 23, 1999

It was into this volatile situation that Professor Fatima Meer came in 1999 to share the good news of a better life for all with the people of Chatsworth. Instead, the residents asked her to listen to them. They showed her their dilapidated homes, they showed her their rent slips that contained a baffling myriad of charges, and made their own charge that their lives were steadily getting worse. The local councilors' only relationship to the community was to encourage them to pay up or get out. As one of the CCG delegation remembers, it was also a challenge that the residents threw out. They demanded that the CCG members free themselves from the shackles of the vote, of sectarian loyalist politics, and conservative economic policies.

Abandoning the quest for votes, the CCG started to transform itself into a human rights pressure group. It acted as a catalyst for reinvigorating flat dwellers' associations in Units 2, 3, and 10. A powerful leadership started to emerge in these areas, some relying on the grounding they had received as shop stewards in the union movement of the 1980s. Through all this the council continued to send out reams of eviction notices.

The most organized areas seemed to be targeted in an attempt to engender fear and division. Rival civic associations were sponsored among the well-to-do on the outskirts of the sub-economic units, who were told they could purchase flats once the current owners were moved out. The city council started to demonize the CCG as being anarchists and the like. These tactics were reminiscent of the apartheid period.

A series of meetings was held at which the CCG, together with residents, devised methods of staving off any new attempt at eviction. Rumors were rife of frenzied preparation by council officials to clamp

down, once and for all, on the Chatsworth civic associations. The more
the protests intensified, the more the council was baited into incredible
callousness. An 88-year- old granny, Begam Govindsamy, was given notice
of eviction. During the apartheid era, she had twice been evicted, the
first time from Fynnland and the second from Clairwood. The press was
becoming critical. It was the likes of Vidu Vedlankar, of DHAC fame, who
were the most vicious in processing these evictions in the rigid fashion of
"I am just following policy."

Meanwhile the community were devising new methods of struggle.
They decided to strike first before evictions happened. In August 1999, residents boarded three buses on a rainy night and protested at the houses of
local councilors. One of them, the NNP's Haniff Hoosen, called the police
and a tense stand off ensued. He claimed to have been slapped by someone
in the crowd during the protest. Protesters left with promises to be back.
Hoosen subsequently moved out of the area. The CCG coordinated the dis-
tribution of food hampers to the indigent. Gangsters who preyed particularly on women, both old and young, were "spoken to" and instructed to
mend their ways and move their operations away from the flats environment. Most did. Civic associations were reformed, constitutions meticu-
lously adopted and leaders elected. Care was also taken to have people
deployed to other community organizations, particularly community
policing forums, which turned out to be enormously important structures
in which to have intelligent representation.

And there was time for fun. Diwali, the Hindu festival of lights, was cele-
brated. The festival had a relevant bent. The slogan raised was "lights for all"
and the Satanic villain was cast as the city council, which was disconnecting lights. Old mythologies from India were being reinterpreted in neo-liberal Africa. All religious groups and races living in the mosaic of
Chatsworth participated. Indeed, about 30 percent of the area is African
and strong bonds between neighbors were being forged in the context of
the struggle against the city council. In this way, Diwali in South Africa was
being rethought, politicized, and made accessible to all the community.

Over time the civic associations developed a common set of demands.
They wanted their arrears to be wiped out, evictions to be stayed, water and
electricity to be reconnected, and the flats to be upgraded. They took an
important defensive initiative by taking the council to court to prevent evictions. They argued that the state's so-called Masakhane campaign was at
variance with the provision in the constitution that guaranteed human dig-

nity, a right to shelter for them and their children, and access to sufficient water and nutrition. They argued that the state was prevented from ejecting people from their homes unless suitable alternative accommodation existed. As such measures did not exist, magistrate after magistrate issued interdicts stopping proposed evictions. The press cottoned onto this unusually militant and effective campaign. Council bureaucrats pulled out their hair.

THE DURBAN METRO COUNCIL changed tack. They adopted a clever and insidious new strategy by trying to force and entice the tenants to take ownership of the houses. They used the existence of a R7,500 government subsidy to discount the price of the houses. As they became more desperate to transfer ownership, they constantly reduced the valuations of the flats until the price was, unsurprisingly, R7,500. Pamphlets were sent out. Residents could have their houses for free. There would be no more rent to pay. Before this could happen, however, each block, housing six or more families, would have to form a corporate body. What people were not told was that they had to pay their arrears in full, and would have to pay rates and levies equal to rental. And once corporate bodies were formed, constitutional fetters to evicting people would no longer apply. These would become civil matters, where the sheriff could eject people on behalf of the banks or other property owners without regard to the "human dignity" and other fundamental rights of indigent persons. As things stood—that is, if tenants did not take ownership of the houses—the council would be required to provide alternative accommodation, which it did not have. Also by getting rid of the houses that it rented out and for which it had to collect rent, the council would remove an important mobilizing subject. The historical role council played as landlord would be annulled.

In essence, by privatizing living arrangements, collective memories of struggle would be replaced by the immediacy of dealing with banks and other lending institutions as individuals. Pockets would be gentrified and the council security forces would make way for the body corporate as the disciplining agent. This fracturing of the collective feeds into making the processes of exploitation, control, and surveillance more subtle, diffused and effective.59

And so one steamy Saturday morning, in November 1999, a council entourage rolled into Westcliff. They arrived with a phalanx of bureaucrats, a photocopy machine, and pieces of paper on official letterheads. They decamped at a school in Unit 3, not to evict but to sign over houses to tenants who in turn would sign mortgages and settle all their arrears. The transfer of homes was to be presented as a purely technical affair. A huge armed force of council security guarded the room with the photocopy machine. But by now the community was alive to the implications of this tactic. A violent confrontation ensued as 300 protesters arrived. But they were not against the sale of houses. Famously, one of the leaders of the march shouted, "Viva Title Deeds, Viva!" The demand was for a commitment from the council to first upgrade the houses and then for their transfer, irrespective of arrears.

The irony was that many of the leaders who gathered at a mass meeting in Chatsworth in 1980 and had argued that the houses in Unit 3 did not have a shelf life of more than 15 to 20 years, were now trying to force the selfsame houses upon the residents. Now they were present as highly paid council employees and councilors. After the protesters had spent two hours encircling the room in which the photocopying machine was kept, the process was forced to a stop. It had become clear to officials that there were no takers for that deal.

As the Council officials retreated, a defining moment in the struggle for Chatsworth occurred. One of the designer-bedecked (African) councilors began castigating the crowd. She had once lived in a shack, she screamed. Why were Indians resisting evictions and demanding upgrades? Indians were just too privileged. One elderly aunty, Girlie Amod, screamed back: "We are not Indians, we are the poors." The refrain caught on as councillors hurried to their cars. As they were leaving they would have heard the slogan mutate as Bongiwe Manqele introduced her own good humored variant, "We are not African, we are the poors." Identities were being rethought in the context of struggle and the bearers of these identities were no respecters of authority.

The particular kind of identity congealing in this moment had no grand ideological preconditions and so could not be co-opted by government sloganeering. It was organized around the primary realization that resistance had to be offered against the hostilities being visited on the poor. Attempts to head off militance by the local ANC were easily fobbed off. The residents showed flexibility in constantly shifting the goalposts of what it would take for them to accept the title deeds, such as the demand for upgrading, writing off of arrears, and the forming of body "co-operatives." The ANC, hemmed in by its own economic conservatism, could not match this flexibility.

Notwithstanding these dangers, there were many people interested in this "deal." Some were relatively well-off or had children who had done well for themselves, who saw a chance to own a flat for free. However, the allure of the discourse of private ownership was felt even in the executives of the flat residents associations. Initially, the CCG tried to argue that private property was anathema to a sense of community and pointed out that the council still demanded a settlement of unpayable arrears and that rates and levies were but another kind of rent. Still, the idea of ownership, no matter how punishing the mortgage taken to pay off arrears, was passionately received. The CCG learned quickly that resistance was not only about sponsoring a discourse that ran counter to that of the state.

7. upgrading the houses and the return of relocation

ONCE THE COUNCIL indicated its desire to expedite the transfer of houses and the leadership of the flat dwellers realized that many people were anxious to own their homes, the demand mutated. Now the emphasis shifted to the upgrading of the hovels. An independent civil engineering consultant was called in by the flat residents' associations to assess the flats. The report listed the defects found in most buildings:

1. Water penetration at the junction of the external wall with floor slabs was evident.

2. Water penetration through the external walls results in ponding on the internal floors.

3. Roof sheets needed replacing.

4. The water supply pipes in the flats were generally rusted, furred up, and in a poor state of disrepair, requiring replacement. The bulk underground water reticulation was of badly corroded galvanized pipe. There were chronic water leaks. Under general observations, the report found that there was a general lack of maintenance, poorly maintained public places and pitifully few amenities.

The costs of the refurbishing was easily recoverable from the R7,500 per household subsidy that the central government had made available to first-time homeowners. The council had other ideas. It argued that the flats would be sold at R7,500 but presented this as if they were giving the flats away for free, estimating the value of the flats at exactly R7,500! However, it was discovered that the law required the flats to be upgraded before the transfer in terms of the Discount Benefit Scheme, in particular Section 4.4.1, outlined in the Implementation Manual.

Once again the council was thwarted by legality, if only a temporary technical impediment. But they stuck to their guns on the vital question of arrears. All arrears had to be settled for a sale to occur. Those who could not settle their arrears either by paying up or by securing a bank mortgage would, council officials vaguely threatened, be relocated.

Meanwhile the provincial Department of Housing which had jurisdiction over the nearby Shallcross flats began to upgrade these flats. The province envisaged transferring the flats to the local sphere of government. The council, through the director of housing, Nonhlanhla Mthembu, was adamant that this would not happen. Her rationale was that this would make transparent the council's failure to upgrade other flats, such as those in Bayview and Westcliff, as the Shallcross flats would have been completed by then. This frustration of delivery led to an amazing spat between the provincial and local council housing authorities.

In a letter, the director of asset management in the Provincial Housing Department, recorded Mthembu's response to the proposal to transfer the Shallcross flats in the following manner: "Her response was that she could not see her way clear in accepting such a proposal because, if Metro Council did take over the Shallcross flats then it would seem as if the Metro Council would be applying double standards. She pointed out that the Shallcross flats were in the process of being upgraded by the Department whilst other flats in the ownership of the Council are not undergoing a similar exercise." In the contorted logic of bureaucrats, delivery had become a bad thing, something to be avoided lest expectations be created!

REELING FROM DEFEATS in the law courts and at the mass level, the council, through the voice of the deputy mayor, Trevor Bonhomme, began to threaten relocation of indigent people to "starter homes." These were literally the size of toilets flung even further from the city center. The residents who had struggled so long to build a sense of community and a fledgling non-racialism were to be uprooted again. Ironically it was many of the African residents who would suffer. Relocation, the apartheid discourse, was now part of the language of the ANC. According to Bonhomme poor people could not be given any leeway because this "could be construed as condonation of the culture of non-payment" (*Rising Sun*, August 10–16, 1999).

One of the central reasons for raising the specter of relocation was because the indigents were seen as a barrier to the council off loading the houses as quickly as possible at a tidy profit. A Metro Council memorandum pointed out that "one cause of the inability to sell is that in terms of Council policy and the Discount Benefit Scheme, indigent tenants who are in arrears are unable to take advantage of the Discount Benefit Scheme until they have settled their debts with Council. In addition, in the majority of instances, a residual amount is still payable after the Discount Benefit Scheme grant and indigent tenants are unable to afford this in many cases."[1] Very clearly the council's public pronouncement that the selling of houses would benefit the poor was debunked by their own internal memoranda. The community, in fact, would be divided with the not-so-poor staying behind and the poor forced out.

Maurice Makhatini, the acting executive director of housing, explained that the relocation envisaged by the council was not apartheid: "Apartheid was about grouping races. This proposal is about grouping classes. Those in the same economic bracket will obviously stay together. It is racially blind. Normal business practice demands that if tenants can't pay rent, they must be evicted."

There was immediate reaction from the community organizations most at threat. The leader of the Westcliff Flat Residents Association, Orlean Naidoo, was cutting: "In the past we were moved because of race, now we are being forced out because we are poor. Is this not discrimination? Instead of compensation for the pain and suffering we suffered under apartheid, we're being exposed to humiliation, violence and evictions under the new government." The CCG, through their spokesperson, Iqbal Meer Sharma, immediately threatened mass action vowing never to let relocation happen (*Sunday Tribune*, May 21, 2000). The CCG hosted a series of meetings in Chatsworth and planned a march to city hall. Professor Meer also made a call to her brother, Farouk Meer, an ANC Councilor, and vice-chair of the housing committee, warning of the dire consequences should relocation be attempted.

On Monday, June 12, 2000, the housing committee of council met to discuss the Housing Department's proposal of relocation. The proposal recommended that tenants be relocated without any choice as to where they were going. The newly dispossessed would leave with less than nothing. They would have to sign legally enforceable acknowledgments of debt in respect of past debt incurred. Defending the proposal, Maurice Makhatini argued that the policy was developed in response to a mandate from central councilors and was part of a project to "right- size" housing allocations. Farouk Meer warned that the issue of relocation "would be met with much resistance," accurately predicting that popular opposition to relocations could unleash forces not easily controlled in a year of local government elections (*Natal Mercury*, June 13, 2000). The Metro councilors agreed to defer the decision until their respective parties had caucused on the issue.

But by this time a tide of resentment against ANC councilors had arisen. Some in the ruling party could not understand their fall from grace except in conspiratorial terms. They could not accept that their ideas had been discredited. Deputy Mayor Trevor Bonhomme accused the CCG of being counterrevolutionary and of "using the poor." This labeling echoed the abuse suffered by activists of the 1960s, who were called agitators and users of the poor for political ends. The demands that the residents were making were exactly the demands that Bonhomme had made as the spokesperson of DHAC in the 1980s.

Bonhomme also accused the CCG and in particular Professor Meer of defending Indian privilege, a charge echoed by the youthful Lucky Gabela of the ANC's regional office who was still in his teens when Mandela was released. However, the rank and file of the ANC, such as it still exists, were clearly on the flat dwellers' side. In addition, some middle-ranking officials gave valuable, if private, moral support. But the ANC leadership was bewildered. Nothing demonstrated how seriously they took the Chatsworth uprisings better than their extraordinary paranoiac behavior when the communities invited Winnie Mandela to speak. She agreed, but the regional office, in hysterical telephone calls and letters, prevailed upon her not to come, arguing that she would be supporting extra-parliamentary, sectional, and ethnic politics. This accusation was received with some mirth coming as it did from a party that was in a formal alliance with the ethnically–based Minority Front (MF) and that had abandoned the suburb of Havenside in a by- election held at the time to the MF.

1   Durban Metro Council, *Policy on Rightsizing of Indigent Tenants* (2000).

8. is it legal to be poor?: evictions and resistance

The evictions had nothing to do with non-payment of rent,
but their illegal activity . . . The Council agreed
that evictions of illegal occupants and those involved
in unseemly behavior continue as normal.

—TREVOR BONHOMME, deputy mayor

Is it a coincidence that the minute we organize
independent civics that challenge the Council, Bonhomme
pulls out the card that reads shebeen owners and drug lords.
His allegations criminalize the whole community.

—BRANDON PILLAY, community activist

SO FAR, there had been two attempts at evictions, one every two years. The new century opened with an assault on what the council called "illegals." This was to be the discourse cloaking a third round of evictions. There were two kinds of illegals; those who could not pay and those who were "undesirable." The latter were labeled by Bonhomme as drug lords, shebeen owners and, by a senior official of the council, as "sexual deviants." Deputy director of Housing Mthembu never explained what she meant although a rather forlorn smile played upon her lips as she made the accusation. Three "undesirable" families were targeted.

Mr. Biswanath lives in Unit 3. He has occupied his flat for over 12 years. An epileptic, his seizures became more frequent and he could no longer live independently. He invited his niece, Vanessa Pillay, to stay with him in August 1999. She is married with three children—a eleven-year-old girl, a nine-year-old boy, and a seven-year-old boy who suffers from severe asthma. When she moved in, a white official, Mr. Swart, told her that she could only live with one of her children. The eleven- and nine-year-olds went to live with her father. She was sad that she could not watch them grow.

Vanessa and her husband operate a cosmetics stand at the Bangladesh market on weekends. During the week her husbands sells these items door to door. They survive on the R500 this brings in a month. Here notions of the romance of self-employment are quickly dispelled. The informal economy is about eking out an existence. Barely.

On February 9, 2000, Mr. Biswanath's home was targeted for eviction. This time the council was taking no chance of being outnumbered. A large column of some ten police vehicles and two platoons of armed men followed the sheriff of the court. Firing tear gas, they entered the premises. Mr. Biswanath suffered a seizure. All the goods were thrown out of the flat. R400 was stolen from the flat. Professor Meer arrived at the scene as the last of the Biswanath's and Pillay's possessions were being thrown out. Unable to reason with the officials she called on the people to passively resist by lying across the road. But the violent deed had been done. So she sought legal help to reverse the eviction while sending an "advanced guard" of resisters to the next site of eviction.

The experience left Vanessa shattered: "Since that day, I don't know what it is to have a meal without thinking about it—the fear hasn't left me . . . Every time we hear a sound outside, we become very scared, thinking they are coming again." If Vanessa and her family are evicted, they literally have nowhere to go—the houses of friends and family she might rely on are filled beyond capacity. Under pressure to justify their actions to the media, the council retreated from Bonhomme's wild accusations of "undesirability." The official reason forwarded by the council for eviction is not the labels Bonhomme attaches, but because the Pillays have no permission to live with their "uncle."

ON THE SAME DAY the sheriff arrived at Mr. Mhlongo's residence in Unit 2. He has lived in the flat for eight years. He is a self-employed mechanic, and a single father of two boys and two girls. The sheriff was backed by the same large force of council security, but now reinforced by a division of the Public Order Policing (POP). The reason for the force was the spontaneous mobilizations the day before when the sheriff and council security had attempted to evict Mhlongo. Then a group of over 150 people, mainly women, had driven them away from the Mhlongo residence. This time there were more police than people. Nevertheless, the community blockaded the narrow flight of stairs that led to Mhlongo's flat. What the people lacked in numbers, they made up for in concentration. One group was thronged six rows deep all the way up the stairwell. Smaller groups of onlookers-cum-protesters orbited the police, keeping them busy with catcalls and argument on the fringes of their position. Meanwhile the CCG's legal representatives were rushing to court to interdict the evictions. The lawyer, Siven Samuels, sent out word to organize revenue stamps. It was obvious a court order was being sought. Iqbal Meer Sharma asked the commanding officer to give the dispute time to be decided one way or the other in the courts, before moving in. It would mean holding off any violent police action for 30 minutes. The commander indicated that the "boss" at city hall had refused to allow any delay. Meer Sharma relayed this information to the protesters. Suddenly everyone became quiet, but resolute. Children were shoved out of the way as the commanding officer ordered the storming of the stairwell. The security forces moved in. All hell broke loose.

Journalist Veven Bisetty, writing in the local morning paper, described

a scene reminiscent of a small-scale war. Gunshots ringing out every few minutes, policemen on every corner with rifles at the ready, teargas hanging in the air. But this was no war-torn country. It was Bayview in Chatsworth, where residents resorted to violent battles with Durban Metro Council security officials and their allies, members of the SAPS, who were attempting to evict illegal tenants occupying council dwellings. There were at least six casualties in this latest skirmish, but the battle lines have been drawn. The residents have vowed to prevent evictions from taking place. (*Natal Mercury*, February 10, 2000)

It is still unclear why the police started shooting live ammunition. But whatever their reason, they never expected such a fierce response from the community. Their first baton charge was repelled and people who, up until now, were mere onlookers, were so infuriated at the brutality they witnessed that they too entered the fray. It was no longer a "battle for Mhlongo, but for our human dignity. We are not animals to be treated like this," said Jooma, a resident shot in the head during the 30-minute fracas.

Radio journalist Ragini Archary was also hit in the head. She drew her hand away from her forehead to reveal a gaping wound, an image beamed across South Africa on television news later that day. Another local resident was lucky to be alive after apparently being hit by a ricocheting bullet. Although the casualties were high, the ferocity and dedication of the community forced the security forces to call for further backup in order to retreat from the area, without effecting the eviction.

This was another defining moment for the struggle of the flat dwellers. Indian women had stood in the line of fire in order to protect an African family who had no mother. If they had lost, the Mhlongos would have been forced into the nearby bush. The council, too, had shown its hand. For them the broader issues of the sense of building non-racial communities from the bottom up meant nothing. The fact that Mhlongo was respected by the community and was working hard as a mechanic to give his family a chance in life was equally irrelevant. The council was a debt collector, fighting on moral terms. Their sense of morality was frighteningly clear. Mhlongo was an undesirable because he got in the way of their collection of (apartheid's) debts.

The third family on the eviction list was that of Sukdeo (Ricky) and Salvarani (Pearl) Jankipersadh. They have three children including five-year-old twins. Ricky is employed with a transportation company that removes rubbish. They lived in a tuck shop that had no water and lights for two years. Pearl tells of sending her six year old to school late because she had to wait for her neighbor's family to go to work before her son could use their toilet and bathroom. Snakes had also entered the tuck shop, nestling in the grooves of the corrugated iron floor. After noticing a vacant flat they moved in. They had been on the waiting list for nine years and had given up all hope of getting a home through the normal channels. The council's response was that they wanted to place somebody else in the house. Fair enough. What then happens to the Jankipersadhs? The council's plan, as revealed through an internal memorandum, was that evictions would "serve to some small degree to reduce the housing backlog."[1] Responds Meer Sharma: "Surely the answer is to build more houses rather that evicting one family and inserting another and in this way creating the illusion of housing people."

Luckily, the fierce reaction of the communities meant that the council dared not attempt to evict this family. By the time the police contingent sped out of Bayview under a hail of stares and under the glare of television cameras—to have the magazines in their firearms examined by an irate station commander whose telephones were already jammed by calls from the press and members of the community—an interdict against evictions had, anyway, been granted.

After the interdicts were granted, the council got their media machine up and running. In an aggressive response, the Metro Council "anticipated" the interdict the CCG had obtained that stopped the evictions of three "illegal" tenant families. Waiving their right to more time to respond to the CCG's founding papers, the council quickly fired off affidavits denying they were doing anything wrong and demanding that the court dispense with the matter at an earlier date. On television, they lambasted the three tenants at risk of eviction as being "shebeen owners," "drug lords," and, once again, "sexual deviants." No longer is it enough for there to be agitators and anarchists misleading people. The people are the problem themselves. A law clerk taking statements from the three families was initially outraged that the residents had been so "insulted." He suggested "defamation" suits. Someone else doubted whether the council knew that they were lying. Just as in the past, it was to be presumed that poverty-stricken township dwellers were social deviants by virtue of their degraded circumstances.

THE COUNCIL GOT THEIR DAY IN COURT. So did 200 members of the community who sat jam-packed in the Chatsworth regional court on Tuesday, February 22, 2000. Overnight, the CCG had managed to mount a reply to the council's sneak rebuttal, which right or wrong in law, introduced sufficient legal disputes so that the matter could not go ahead. In order that the point was not missed, and the money spent on buses for transport not wasted, protesters decided, after court was adjourned, to visit the deputy mayor at his well-appointed home. There they would request that he resign for betraying his constituency.

Deputy Mayor Moopanaar was constantly on the search for a political home. He had recently crossed over from the MF to the ANC and had once flirted with the PAC. He was not at his residence. There was, though, a huge police presence. They declared the gathering illegal and threatened to arrest people. People presented themselves to the police vans for arrest.

Suddenly someone grabbed the loud hailer and spoke about Mohammed and the mountain. Idioms are always impressive in mass situations. Everyone seemed to inspire everyone else. Buses were boarded. As those in charge of city council rental stock would not come to the people, the people proceeded to the rent offices. Over one hundred people just walked in to this fortress-like two story building opposite the Chatsworth Shopping Centre while people were paying their bills. They began chanting. Council clients scurried out and the building was theirs. More police arrived. They gave protesters an ultimatum to move or forcefully be moved. This contingent of policemen stood half in and half outside the building. Suddenly somebody had the bright idea to close the doors. Automatically bolts slammed shut. There was a stand off. The policemen outside debated whether this was now a "hostage situation." Were their colleagues inside "in control" or had they been disarmed? The deputy mayor, Moopanaar, and head of housing, Joe Nene were sent for over the cell phone, walkie-talkie, and landlines inside the building where many staff were now holed up. These officials arrived. Just as well. Some kind of countdown was going on inside the building. 60, 59, 58, 57, 56, 55. Somewhere between 6 and 0, the mayoral entourage slunk in. The heavy doors swung open, the crowd surged to meet him, and Moopanaar was immediately told to resign. Visibly shaken, he conceded a moratorium on evictions "until the end of the month," during which time, the council, though committed to cost- recovery, would "look into the matter further." An old man stated that no one believed Moopanaar anymore but that they, the protesters, had made their point. They promised that they would be back if evictions were attempted again.

The next time, three weeks later, the three families appeared in court, the magistrate did not. The community left the courtroom and linked up with some 2,000 mainly African protesters from nearby Bottlebrush who were angry about the racism and corruption of police in the area.

Finally the three families had their day in court. A strong police presence took the back rows of the court. It was decided to deal with the Jankipersadhs first as it was felt to be the most difficult of the cases for the CCG's legal representatives. In a case (brilliantly argued) by the CCG's legal representatives, Shanta Reddy and Siven Samuels, the council was prevented from evicting the Jankipersadhs. The magistrate found that the "City Council did not follow the due process of the law and thus found itself in a predicament in the present case." The council lost with an award of costs against it. Faced with growing outrage in the community, the council established a commission of inquiry to investigate how the police force and council security personnel had acted unlawfully, with such deadly force.

1   Durban Metro Council, *Policy on Rightsizing of Indigent Tenants* (2000).

9. faces in the crowd

The changes made by ANC women in politics were striking—
they ranged from toilets for women and a creche
in Parliament to a commitment of female cabinet ministers
towards bettering the lives of women on the ground.

—ANTJIE KROG, *Mail and Guardian*, August 4, 2000

AT ALMOST EVERY MASS MEETING a young woman would sit impassively with a child on her knee. She never spoke but was ever present. She was always wore a slightly faded blue punjabi. Then all of a sudden she stopped coming. I traced her back to a flat she shared with six other people and asked her to tell me her story. It came pouring out.

Shoba was 22 years old. Her son was born when she was 14. She was raped by the son of her mother's new lover. Nobody wanted to listen. Periodically her rapist would return to taunt her and for sex.

She got a job at a clothing factory in Clairwood. A bit of independence came from the money. A bit of freedom too. But it made the "brother" angry. He tried to burn down the house. He broke the windows. She got a restraining order. He stabbed her. She retreated further into the house. Always hiding. She had no income. At the welfare office they told her that her son was too old to qualify for a grant. Her son went hungry. It was no wonder that he still clung to his mother at the age of eight.

She got another job, this time at Unit 10 in Chatsworth. A clothing factory called Staying Alive. But he worked downstairs. He grabbed her pay packet. He laughed at the restraining order. The police said Shoba must telephone when he was around or she must bring him to the police station. She left the job.

She stopped coming to the mass meetings because she had found another job. In Unit 10 again. Seven days a week at R150. From 7:00 A.M. to 6:20 P.M. Often they worked till 8:20 P.M. No overtime is paid.

She lives in constant fear of him. He has acquired a mythical reputation of appearing and just as quickly disappearing. Two weeks before Woman's Day he saw her at the local market. He tried to stab her with a broken bottle. Her friend intervened in a bid to protect her and was stabbed herself.

The mass meetings were a refuge. But the power generated there could not help her confront and overcome her enemy. The mainly female leadership sympathized. They clicked their tongues. She smiled ruefully. The news was that somewhere, somehow, he had received a hiding. Would he be back?

ANNELINE GANESH WOKE UP on the morning of March 24, 2000, full of adolescent expectation. Fifteen years of age, she had planned to attend her first "last-day matinee" disco. She had no intention of going to school as no work was done on the last day. Taking time over her dressing, she linked up with her friends barely able to contain her excitement. They first spent some time at the Chatsworth Center before making their way to the Throb nightclub.

It was Friday. The matinee was due to start at 1 P.M. and they arrived at 12:25. Already the queue was long. The entrance fee was R12. By the time she got inside the place was overflowing with kids intent on having a good time. Anneline danced for a short while. It was extremely hot and she made her way to the stairs to get some fresh air. Suddenly she was swept up in an inexplicable stampede. She tried to keep pace with the flow of kids but lost her shoes and slipped. Kids ran over her. Anneline saw knees and ankles all around her, their bodies piling up next to her. She lost consciousness just as she felt the pain of bones snapping in her legs. She tried to wake up but could not move. Two guys lying next to her called people to take her out. She saw the flesh above her hip split open. Her leg lay limp.

Almost two months after the tragedy that claimed 13 young lives I visited Anneline at her home. She has steel pins inserted into her legs at grotesque angles. She lives on the third floor of their rented accommodation in Unit 10. Her mother is at work. She managed to find work at a clothing factory in central Durban. She is 34 years old. Already she faced the specter of short- time as the clothing industry suffers a continuing loss of jobs. Tariff barriers have come tumbling down. Her husband abandoned them when Anneline was very young. He did visit once after the tragedy.

Anneline's grandparents have stood in. Her grandfather, Govindsamy Naidoo, grew up in the Bayside area near Clairwood. His parents farmed cabbages. Anneline's grandmother, Mariamma, lived in Wentworth. Her

father was a fisherman. They moved to Chatsworth in 1972. Grandpa
Govindsamy worked at Hind Brothers and after the company moved to
Johannesburg, he found part-time work at R.K. Khan's hospital. He was
"boarded" because of ill-health. In the 1970s Mariamma found work at
Olympic Clothing in Clairwood. That company also closed down. They are
worried about the transfer of the flats to private ownership. They were
enthusiastic at first but are worried that the levy will be too high. "Just
another form of rent," says Govindsamy, turning up his hands. As it is, the
rent, lights and water amounted to R600.

The third-floor flat has become a prison for Anneline. Even if she was
helped downstairs, there is no transport to take her anywhere. What she
does not realize is that her family is going to find it difficult to hold on to the
flat that has become her prison. If the clothing industry continues its downward spiral, her mother will be placed on longer and longer periods of short-
time. Keeping the flat, whether rented or "owned," will become a miracle.

It says a lot about the mood of the time that a social movement should
arise as a result of a luridly named "disco tragedy." The Throb deaths galvanized the community. Residents, activists, and political parties formed the
Chatsworth Community Distress Committee. Funds were raised to support
the affected families and a memorial service was held. Indeed many memorial services were held. These brought together larger numbers of people
than any mobilization since the protests against the tricameral parliament
in the 1980s. Although not a fraction as politicized as earlier events, the
sheer scale was testimony to the desire of people to control their increasingly desperate lives. The possibility of sustaining a social movement for
the moral upliftment of Chatsworth was raised by former community
activists like Roy Padayachee, who reemerged as a leader after losing out in
a bruising political battle with the NIC cabal in the years gone by.

Among the leadership of the distress committee, there seemed to be a
reticence about even using the word "poverty," let alone pointing to how
the government's macro-economic policy was creating unemployment
and desperation. No accusations were directed at the council for refusing
to upgrade the area or provide safe recreational facilities and for cutting
off lights and water. In fact, various mayors were guests of honor at the
memorial service, pathetically jockeying for prime television coverage for
their act of mourning.

The ANC constituency MP for Chatsworth, Ebrahim Ebrahim, writing in
a commemorative publication of the CCDC went so far as to blame the

community themselves, holding that "When children are involved in any tragedy blame for that tragedy must always lie within the broader community." The broader community Ebrahim defined as Chatsworth, which must "put greater effort as a community to provide for the young adults so that they may find places where they can associate with their peers in safety." This attempt to blame the victim was received with antipathy by the crowd. In contrast, the one speaker who did criticize the government and talk about social neglect and marginalization of the youth received frenzied applause from a soccer stadium full of people.

While the meetings of the CCDC were marked by a lack of youth participation, the organization did serve as a catalyst for the development of a number of youth movements. The Rory Youth Movement, named after one of the children who was killed at the Throb, has its origins in Unit 3. The chair of the Bayview Flat Residents Association, 19- year-old Brandon Pillay, emerged as a key figure in the building of a Chatsworth Youth Movement, of which he was eventually elected chairperson. This was a concrete sign that the poor of Chatsworth had started to establish a presence beyond their own constituencies. More important, they were raising the causes of their plight: escalating rent and service charges, the eroding of welfare benefits, and the lack of jobs.

In my own interviews, conducted at the end of 1999 with some 60 youngsters, a pattern started to emerge. The world they occupy is the shopping mall, the badly lit street corner, the video arcade, the disco, and loose groupings of youth who are constantly on the move from house to house, television station to television station with no set destination. They have created a world where adults are absent. Over 80 percent indicated that they have no respect for adults anymore. Gone are the days when any older person was an "uncle" whom one would greet politely.

Adults, particularly men, according to them, are a big disappointment. They are drunks, fools, abusers, cheats. The police aren't to be trusted, politicians sell out, teachers are "in it for the money," and preachers care more about the collection plate than the flock. And since most women are forced—or allow themselves—to be defined in relation to their men, there is a vague sense of disgust toward many "aunties," particularly from young girls themselves. The "responsible" parents are preoccupied with survival. Daddy is not able to fulfill the role as provider he has set for himself. Trying to assert his authority violently only sends the children to seek refuge outside the home. In this atmosphere, traditional family outings, trips to the movies and city center, never happen. Parents occupy a desperate and harsh world separate from their children.

The youth bemoan the death of quality schools and the fact that the school is a set of classes devoid of any social activities. Many spoke of the need for recreation centers that allowed them to socialize, without the determining factor of money. There is an undercurrent of hopelessness. Above all, the youth felt nobody was listening. They felt devalued, dismissed, and degraded at every turn. What did it matter if one excelled at something or other. Some jealous neighbor would eventually notice and immediately drag you down. With over 50 percent unemployment, it is hard to convince the youth that there are options beyond unemployment. Some girls, one just 12 years old, speak openly about getting "sugar daddies" and confess that they won't date anyone who is not well-off, for fear of becoming "hustlers" like their parents.

At home, living conditions are not conducive to healthy interaction anyway. Most people in Chatsworth live in poky homes that leak, with unlit hallways and no parks. Because housing is built on steep slopes, gardening is made difficult and available living space reduced. Homes are no less dangerous than shopping malls and I was surprised at just how desensitized the youth are to violence. Most women suffer "hidings" quite regularly, either from fathers, elder siblings, lovers, or rivals.

Very clearly the state is not going to act. In his speech at the memorial service Minister Kader Asmal wondered why the community was not using school premises to a greater extent to conduct activities and so build more wholesome lives. What he failed to consider was how the schools that his policies had rendered derelict, with no electricity, no security, no cleaning services, could serve as these vaunted community centers. Metro Mayor Obed Mlaba could not bring himself to explain how his council had frittered away hundreds of thousands on celebrating the new millennium. Similarly, nothing was said about how the escalating costs of social services hurt the poorest of the poor and how child-care grants are slashed while millions of rands in the welfare budget are left unspent. Nor was much attention spent trying to understand the subjective condition of being a youth today. The response to the Throb tragedy was, by and large, sanctimonious, old-fashioned, and very uncool.

Although short-lived, the intense response that kept 100 activists mobilized for a month shows the potential for issue-based social movements which mobilize stadiums full of people. It is these organizations that responded to the tragedy. And it is these structures that are starting to regain the confidence to wage mass struggles, which pierce the rhetoric of ministers and mayors and proffer demands that address the root cause of the social distress in townships like Chatsworth.

WHILE THE YOUTH IN GENERAL are disaffected, the children in the sub-economic flatlands are in serious trouble. There is a strong element of what sociologists have come to label a "culture of urgency." Life is lived in the immediate, made up of a series of separate instances because there is no future, only the present. "So life has to be lived as if each instant were the last one, with no other reference than the explosive fulfillment of indi-vidualized hyperconsumption. This constant, fearless challenge to explore life beyond its present dereliction keeps destitute children going: for a while, until facing utter destruction." [1]

Many get criminalized early in life. Valentino Naidoo is just 13 years old but looks no more than 9. He was caught with a toothbrush in his pocket at a local supermarket. He was taken to a backroom, stripped naked, and beaten. He was then hauled off to the local police station, charged, and released on R300 bail.

When I met Valentino his school pants were held up by a string and his toes stuck through his shoes. He spoke dispassionately about his beating. He admitted taking the toothbrush. Why a toothbrush, I asked. Hesitantly he told me that the girls at school had made fun of him because of bad breath. Valentino's father had long abandoned them and his mother suf-fered from a debilitating psychiatric condition that prevented her from obtaining anything more than casual employment.

CCG lawyer Shanta Reddy took on Valentino's case. She wrote to NICRO. Their reply, dated November 24, 1999, tells its own story:

VALENTINO NAIDOO: Case Number: Unknown

The above-mentioned was referred to our offices for possible inclu-sion into one of our diversion programmes.

The client was assessed and found unsuitable for diversion for the following reasons:

1) His mother is a single parent and unemployed. She cannot afford to send him to our programme in town. Further, due to his age she

cannot send him to town alone and further will not be able to afford additional busfare for herself.

2) The client claims that he stole the toothbrush as he did not have one. This in itself demonstrates the family's financial situation.

In light of the above, we regret that we cannot assist in this matter. We recommend that charges be withdrawn.

Feeding into the destitution is the erosion of the state's safety net. The reduction of what is called the Child Support Grant (CSG) from R420 to R100 and its limitation to children under seven years old has exacerbated hardship for the single mothers of Chatsworth.87 Children are being taken out of school because of their inability to meet school fees or the urgent need to get money through begging or casual employment. Mothers and girls, some as young as 11, have turned to prostitution.

The rise of youth movements after the tragedy might signal a greater understanding of the world that the young occupy. However, there is also the danger of youth organizations becoming part of the conservative back-lash that was evident in the aftermath of the Throb tragedy. Often poverty and the erosion of hope can become fertile recruiting grounds for religious fundamentalists and cultural chauvinists. Those movements already have a significant presence in the area and were quick to use the disco deaths as a platform to demonize the youth and present themselves as the exorcists.

BUT THERE IS A CREATIVE IMPULSE that continues to break through, even in these circumstances. It shows itself when over 1,200 people pack the Odeon Cinema to celebrate National Women's Day on August 9, 2000. Talent from Chatsworth was on display—the Awesome Foursome, dancers from the Zanzibari community, and the rapper Psyches. The hall erupted when Psyches took the stage. After the "incisive" intellectual analysis of the guest speakers, it was the haunting and militant message of rap and hip-hop that got the crowd—from age 3 to age 80—on their feet. A tall, angular, super-cool, and utterly "down" figure, Psyches oozes anti-establishment attitude.

Women of Chatsworth unite
Women lead the fight
Pick up the stones

Break Council's bones
Fatima Meer is in the house
Trevor Bonhomme is a mouse

PSYCHES' LYRICS captured the emergent consciousness and the immediate past battles in a language that people could relate to. The rap came flooding out. Poverty/resistance, evictions/invasions, racism/community, authority/confrontation, city hall/civics. But Psyches can also make you cry. So young and so wise already, Psyches raps about "First Night." This haunting poem laid over atmospheric dub-music tells of the minute preparations made by a person the first time they have to sell their body for money.

Rap artist as the custodian of the people's history. Critical interpreter— not praise singer or agitator, not soothsayer. Artist confronting the truths of the bourgeois media and the spin doctoring of the new elite. The truths of the "poor" flow through the rapper.

Psyches is roaming the townships. A gossiper carrying stories from the "poors" that gather around him. Embellishing here and there, but carrying the rumor, a human pamphleteer.

Certainly Psyches throws a twenty-first century challenge to last century's model of revolutionary propagandist. The latter comes across as a tired figure, otherworldly, one step removed from the everyday rhythms of township life, talking a turgid, frigid language, preaching from on high rather than organizing. Truly these sad, defeatist figures cannot tune into the capacity of the "poors" to organize themselves and help that process along.

While it is crucial to get the demands right in any struggle, Psyches is pointing to the importance of the "messenger" in these new transition times where form and content must once again merge.

1   Manuel Castells, *End of Millennium* (London: Blackwell, 1998), p. 160.

10. Working life: from rags to tatters

Everyday another worker comes to me having just lost a job
or having been put on short-time. Many of the people from my area
found work in the clothing and textile industry in the past.
This industry has already shed tens of thousands of jobs
the last two years. One feels especially sad for the single mothers
who slave away in sweatshops only to be told to leave
after a few years . . . I know that they will never work again
but I choose to give them hope.

—ORLEAN NAIDOO, Chairperson, Westcliff Flat
Residents Association, *Towards Democracy*, 2000

OVER THE YEARS, a large number of men and women from Chatsworth have found work in the clothing and textile industries. For women it was a source of liberation as they broke the taboo on working outside the home and confronted the tradition that assigned them the role of housewife. But it was a double-edged sword. At work they had to labor under the brutal gaze of the male supervisor who acted much like the father-in-law they thought they had escaped. And at home they still had to do the cooking and other household chores. As the cost of living soared, being in the factory became an economic necessity rather than a political act.

As the clothing and textile industries started to shed labor it was the men who went first. Many men became reliant on their wife's wages. Newspaper columnist Gita Pather, who grew up in Westcliff, tells of men waiting for their wives at the bus stop on Friday and forcefully taking hold of their pay packets. Many women opted to be single mothers, often ostracized by family and community, rather than continue to put up with abuse and exploitation.

Since the mid-1990s the downward spiral of the industry has forced many of the women of Chatsworth into unemployment. Both employers and trade unions hold that these job losses are directly related to the state's trade liberalization policies. This involves cutting the tax on imports and ending the protection of industries from outside competition. Since clothing work in other parts of the world is typically done by young children laboring under appalling conditions for slave wages, only a reproduction of these profitable circumstances is likely to make South African jobs competitive. While South Africa was required by the World Trade Organization to phase out its tariffs over 12 years the government volunteered to do it in 8. Whatever one's take on industrial policy, the fact is that tens of thousands of jobs have been lost. In the first six months of 1999 alone, just over 10,000 jobs were jettisoned in and around Durban. Hidden behind the bald statistics lay a lot of ruined lives.

Like those of John and Angie Stephen. John and Angie are both 40 years old. They were childhood sweethearts who married at 17. They traveled to work together, to the same clothing company owned by I.M. Lockhat. Together they spent four decades in the factory. They have two adult children, Samantha, who is married, and Joshua. Both took home R320 a week. They paid R600 to rent a dilapidated one-roomed outbuilding in Westcliff.

Over the years the management was getting more repressive. They remembered fondly the days of the paternalism and benevolence that M.H. Lockhat, the father of the present boss, had displayed. The son was sour and distant and kept demanding more of the workers while trying to erode the benefits workers had accumulated through struggle in the 70s and 80s. He brought in family as sectional heads. But the Stephens were prepared to work even harder because for them it was literally a matter of life or death. Their son Joshua had a serious kidney ailment. The couple had followed the Soobramoney case in the media as it made its way to the Constitutional Court. The question decided by that case was whether the constitutional guarantee of a "right to life" would be violated by taking a patient off kidney dialysis, as a cost-saving measure, knowing that this would lead to the death of the patient. The court's refusal to force the state to provide Soobramoney with the necessary medical care made them realize that it was up to them to provide for Joshua. For three years he was on a dialysis machine. And so every week for three years they spent almost R100 to transport him to the hospital.

Finally, in February 1999, Angie donated one of her kidneys to Joshua. It was a huge operation and Angie was advised to stay home for a year. The financial help promised by the company was not forthcoming and so within two months Angie was back at work. She suffered blackouts but stayed at her station because money was still needed for post-operation care for her son. She had already sacrificed part of her body and was determined not to give up.

In April 2000 the company gave the workers two weeks' leave. Angie welcomed the break since she could talk to the doctors looking after Joshua and rest a little. On May 9, 2000, she and John arrived as usual outside the factory gates at a building that once was the Shah Jehan Cinema. Many of her 500 co-workers were milling around outside. They found the factory closed and were informed that the owners had applied for voluntary liquidation. By pursuing this route the company could save huge sums of money on retrenchment pay. It was not really bankrupt but could use this device to open up a factory in the former homeland of QwaQwa at cheaper labor rates.

The Stephens were devastated. Suddenly they were left with nothing to show for their years of labor. A month after the closure they were still in shock. John spoke about the lifelong friends in the line he would probably never see again. He had forced himself to march against job losses in the huge COSATU stayaway, one day after the company closed down, but his heart was not in it. He felt alone despite the thousands of workers around him. A member of the union for two decades he already feels isolated and abandoned. Union officials only really service those who pay subscriptions.

The Stephens had applied for a house 11 years ago. A week after they lost their jobs a social worker visited. She found the living conditions unhygienic for Joshua and promised to expedite their application for housing. It is a tragic irony that after waiting for 11 years the Stephens might be offered a house when they can least afford it. And what will happen to Joshua when the money runs out and he cannot be sent for treatment any longer?

11. thulisile manqele's water

As much as water is a basic human right there is a cost to recover—
the same with lights—which the Metro Council insist on payment
and if no payment is made the Metro Council disconnects.

—TREVOR BONHOMME, 2000

The cold, contemporary cast of power is couched between the lines
of noble-sounding clauses in democratic-sounding constitutions.

—ARUNDHATI ROY, *The Cost of Living*

SOMETIME IN FEBRUARY 2000, former Minister of Water Affairs Kader
Asmal heard that he was to receive an international award for his heroic
efforts to bring water to the poorest of the poor in South Africa. The financial
reward was in the region of $150,000. At the same time during a lull in the
eviction mobilizations Thulisile Christina Manqele, an unemployed former
domestic worker, was preparing to go to court for a different kind of award.

Thulisile Christina Manqele was jubilant when she received notice that
she had been allocated a flat in Chatsworth. The year was 1992 and Christina was a beneficiary of the demise of the Group Areas Act. She had a job
and the new environment with its close proximity to schools meant that
she could provide a better life for her children. As a single mother (her husband was declared a missing person) the upbringing of the children and
keeping the household going was her responsibility. Just 28, she had
thoughts that she might meet somebody who would be a father to the kids
and a husband.

By the time Thulisile moved into 173 Glenover Road, Block 92, in
Chatsworth she had been in the employ of Mrs. Cilliers, as a domestic
worker, for ten years. The work environment was tough but she persevered
because it kept the family alive and paid the rent. At the beginning of
1995, her health started to deteriorate. She began to suffer pains in the

abdominal area. At first the pains were short and sharp. Christina learnt to suffer silently, to avoid the prying eyes of Mrs. Cilliers. She knew that the price of illness was dismissal. But the pains would last for longer and longer—sometimes for days. There was a mutual parting of the ways with Mrs. Cilliers. After more than a decade of service there was no pension, no month's salary to tide her over, no handshake. After 12 years she did not even know Mrs. Cilliers' first name.

In desperation Thulisile joined the long queue at the local state hospital. The medical doctor could not ascertain the cause of the now excruciating and persistent pain. He did give her medication for high blood pressure though. Her lover, who had promised that he would be there forever, told her that he was moving on. She was too tired to complain. Two years after her first trips to the hospital she began to bleed internally. The three-kilometer journey to the hospital took her almost two hours on foot. She awoke the next day in the hospital to find that her spleen had been removed.

Thulisile lives with her four children, one of whom, six-year-old Toti suffers from severe bouts of asthma. In addition she looks after three other children. Zamani Mkhize, aged one, is the child of her sister Nomusa. Nomusa's new husband threatened to kill the child so Thulisile took responsibility for Zamani. Xolani Manqele, seven years old, is her brother's child. Born in a rural area outside Empangeni, Xolani developed kwashiokhor, a disease caused by malnourishment. In addition Xolani suffers from epileptic fits. Xolani's mother requested that Thulisile look after Xolani so that he could benefit from medical attention at the R.K. Khan Hospital. Seven-year-old Thando is the son of a cousin who prevailed upon Thulisile to look after him so that he would have access to the nearby school. For a time Thando's mother brought groceries. But she stopped visiting. Attempts to contact her have failed. She is feared dead.

Unemployed, Thulisile started to fall behind in her rent, water, and electricity payments. In August 1999 her electricity was cut. And then the unthinkable occurred. In the new year, her water was cut. Thulisile managed to secure water through begging from neighbors. But this source dried up as many of the neighbors had their own water cut off and others were worried that they would not be able to afford the costs of a higher water bill. For a while, Thulisile relied on a leaking pipe and then on collecting rainwater. But the cries of one-year-old Zamani grew more insistent. During Durban's dry season, Thulisile turned to a still-standing stream about 50 meters from her flat. An independent analysis of the water indicated that it contained high counts of Coliforms and E-coli, both of which indicate fecal contamination and the presence of human disease-causing agents, making it unfit for human consumption.

Thulisile would have been just another statistic, but her case was brought to the attention of the CCG via the Westcliff Flat Residents Association. It was decided to bring an urgent application to the High Court to get Thulisile's water reconnected. It would serve as a test case for all other indigent people who had had their water cut. The urgent application was granted on Friday, March 8, 2000.

That night, probably at the time Asmal was contemplating how to spend his reward and with the applause of the international audience still ringing in his ears, Thulisile returned to Unit 3 to a jubilant reception. There were angry slogans too—"Kader is a *maeder* [bastard]," "Minister Aasal for the poor," the people chanted.

THULISILE'S RELIEF was only temporary. On June 28, 2000, Thulisile returned to court to argue the case fully. Advocate Maurice Pillemer, representing Thulisile, relied heavily on the provisions of the Water Services Act. He held that a close reading of the act revealed that the council had acted unlawfully because it had not taken Thulisile's personal circumstances into account before cutting the supply, as the act required. Later he conceded that her request was not for an unlimited water supply but for the six kiloliters of water that the council provided free of charge to everybody, including the rich. How could this also have been stopped in the case of someone who most needed such a concession? The judge, Justice Vivien Niles-Duner, was unmoved. These words were like water off a duck's back. She interrupted to ask whether it was true, as the council alleged, that Thulisile's water supply had been illegally reconnected before. This could not be denied and the judge glowered at Thulisile, sitting on a bench at the back of the court, before calling a recess.

During the break, I went downstairs to hear the end of a robbery case. Two men and a woman were waiting to be sentenced in a case of robbery and theft. The legal representative for the woman made a case for leniency on the basis that she was a single mother of five children. Judge Tshabalala was indignant. He thundered back that if he took socioeconomic circumstances into account he would have to make excuses for half of the country.

Back upstairs, Judge Niles-Duner seemed to give Advocate Malcolm Wallis, for the council, a more amiable hearing as he held forth on the

Constitution and the financial limits to socioeconomic rights. He argued that because the regulations for "basic water supply" in terms of the act had not yet been drawn up by the national ministry, these rights were unenforceable. It was a technical point, but I suppose he had his instructions to argue it. As for our state-of-the-art Constitution, Wallis held that a previous case in which a kidney patient seeking free dialysis treatment was allowed to die indicated that rights were limited by the state's budgetary priorities. Every person I try this line of argument on is quick to point out that this means that reasons to misspend on military hardware and the apartheid debt are beyond court scrutiny and once there is no money left, the same courts can safely deny citizens their basic human rights.

Advocate Pillemer's response was that in the absence of promulgated water regulations, the Constitution provided for "sufficient" water as the right of every citizen. "Sufficient water is more than no water at all. As the Constitution is the supreme law of the land, the concept of sufficient water has to be used in place of the absent regulations to define a basic water supply." It took a while to say all this, and it was time for another break.

I arrived back in time to overhear Advocate Wallis tell his junior counsel a joke. The toilets of the judges' chambers at the Durban High Court have signs affixed above them that read "Judges" and "Secretaries." In case anyone missed the point, Wallis explained the assumption and then uttered a slack-jawed guffaw. The junior, a star-struck black woman, seemed suitably impressed at this gender-sensitive man. The judge entered, Wallis bowed, and with the words "My Lady," continued his attack on Thulisile Manqele, single mother and user of water for which she has no money.

A major theme of the council's argument was that Thulisile was undisciplined and could not be relied upon to control her water consumption. Wallis pointed out that by her own admission she even allowed other indigent families the use of water. I wondered whether the African Renaissance and the idea of *ubuntu*—the much-touted African idea of caring for the community—held any water in this court. My reverie was broken by the interjection of Judge Niles-Duner from the bench to share her memories of the water restrictions during the 1984 drought. She said consumers, then, were expected to monitor their water consumption, otherwise supply was restricted and that gardens could only be watered in the early morning or late afternoon. I wondered how many children the judge had to nourish. I wondered whether the judge had had her spleen pulled out. I wondered what the judge's poor front lawn and empty swimming pool must have looked like. I wondered what the judge would do if a neighbor's three- year-old knocked on the door and asked for some water and then a little bit more.

Seemingly emboldened by the judge's slightly obsequious smiles, Wallis tried to find a way around the policy of providing six free kiloliters per household per month. He argued that, while there was this amount provided gratis to all, the council did not have sufficient resources to police the use of the six free kiloliters in respect of people who were too poor to pay should they consume any more. It was a difficult choice to be made but the court also had to consider 8,000 other households that might want to have their water turned on, merely so that they could have access to free water. For a moment I understood how Alice might have felt in Wonderland.

Pillemer tried the children angle. It was argued that to deny them access to water because there were no means to ensure that only a basic supply was consumed was but to reinvoke a limitation of rights where the Constitution did not allow limitation, in respect of the rights of children. The judge frowned. This, clearly, was going to complicate her ruling. So judgment was reserved. I rushed downstairs to hear the outcome of the robbery case. The woman was sentenced to life imprisonment. The omen was not good for Thulisile. Socioeconomic circumstances did not wash well in these courts.

Central to the argument over access to water, though not raised in the courtroom, was the role of the Umgeni Water Board from which the council purchased its water. The price of water kept escalating. A week after Thulisile's case the board raised its tariff by 13 percent. This led to a cross response from KwaZulu-Natal Finance MEC Peter Miller asking whether Umgeni Water is "truly a lean efficient purveyor of water to the poorest of the poor, or is the public perception of Umgeni as a bunch of self-serving fat cats enjoying the benefits of their water supply monopoly a more accurate reflection?" Miller also pointed to the fact that the board's staff were "generously remunerated" and enjoyed "ultra-luxurious and spacious landscaped premises and garages full of luxury motor cars and 4 x 4s" (*Natal Mercury*, July 4, 2000). Margaret Winter, the Metro Executive Committee chairperson, was also critical of the increase, declaring that "the relationship between council and its bulk water supplier should be one of close public-sector collaboration, rather than that of customer and service provider" (*Berea Mail*, July 7, 2000). The criticism was surprising given the fact that it was in keeping with past increases. And both Miller and Winter are firm adherents of privatization. Miller, in his statement, actually referred, without a hint of irony, to the fact that the council was "a major retailer."

It is worth pausing to consider the Metro Council's claim, on which it trades, that it supplies six kiloliters of water a month for free as a means of helping the poor. In court papers in the Manqele case, a whole wad of newspaper reports were presented to support these claims. Tucked away in the body of one of these news stories, one finds an accidental admission. Quoting the director of Metro Water Services, Neil Macleod, the article states that "When the Council totted up the figures, it found that its costs exceeded the income from these homes because it was costing us more to run an account and bill homes than it was recovering from those who used less than 6 kl. per month."

Clearly, even the amount of free water provided to consumers was calculated with reference to what was commercially advantageous to the council and without reference to the needs of indigent people.

Debriefed after the case was heard, lawyers said they thought the judge would rule against Manqele. She was not a "pristine" candidate as questions hung over her head concerning illegal reconnections and supply to her neighbors. Where would one ever find a person willing to martyr herself and her family so that the lawyers could have a good case? And what help is a precedent that applies only to martyrs? The energy, mobilization, and time put into the Manqele case raised the issue of whether activists can acquire any gains from the practice and language of "human rights."

While a lot more creative litigating could be done in conjunction with mass struggles, the way the "limitation clause" in the Constitution is being trotted out in a range of decisions in the courts, these rights are appearing less and less "fundamental." With the Constitutional Court's doctrine of not interfering with policy decisions that are rational and bona fide (in essence, for them, a procedural enquiry), our era of constitutionalism is difficult to distinguish from the apartheid 1950s. Then too, the highest court in the land merely sent the National Party back to convene a proper meeting to take rational decisions to remove colored voters from the common voters' roll in the Cape. The only difference is that the parliamentary sovereignty of those days has been replaced by a sort of executive sovereignty now and the ideology of apartheid as political determinant replaced by the ideology of the market.

Court cases can often consume energies and deflect from mass mobilization. Losses can have the effect of dampening morale. However, the CCG has shown that legal interventions are crucial defensive weapons that also generate publicity and provide focal points for mobilizations. Publicity generates support from radical and even plain old humanitarian types in the suburbs. Linkages with other communities similarly affected by service cuts have also occurred on the back of court cases. Court cases also have the potential to serve as a lightning rod for similar actions in other areas of the country. The actual benefits of litigation, the CCG lawyers concede, is less romantic but no less effective. Litigation consumes the energies of the other side, ripping aside the mask of political rhetoric and forcing the council to reveal in sworn affidavits the brutality of its anti-poor policies.

While judgement on the Manqele case was being considered, the council attempted water cutoffs in Bayview. This was in violation of the *sub judice* nature of the dispute between residents and the council. On the morning of July 18, 2000, a private company with security personnel trundled into the area. By now, the community knew how to mobilize within minutes. A human wall was formed outside the homes of the affected tenants. The CCG, with lawyer Shanta Reddy in tow, were immediately on the scene. Reddy ascertained that the private company did not have the proper paperwork to legally effect the cutoffs. However the company insisted on going ahead. The CCG rushed off to the local magistrate's court for an interdict. No magistrate wanted to touch the matter.

The local SAPS arrived as the community and the security company squared off. It was bizarre. The police threatened to arrest the personnel from the company if they went ahead. The security company withdrew. There was a mood of elation and militance in the Unit 2 and 3 areas with people dancing in the cul-de-sacs between the rows of flats to music hastily improvised and rap songs made up on the spot by local talent Psyches. This was now the fifth battle in a row they had won against those who would either evict them or cut off their water. Whether it was an outside injunction or resistance from within, the poors of Chatsworth had warded off another attack. Chatsworth was fast becoming a theater of defeat for the Metro Council.

To tie up any loose ends, the CCG sought an order in the High Court the next day. This time it was in the name of the Bayview Flat Residents' Association rather than an individual. At the doors of court an agreement was reached that the water cutoffs would be stopped. A week later a dramatic announcement was made. The council proposed the installation of a water restriction device that would allow for precisely 200 liters to be consumed a day. Accounts would be frozen with no further interest charged on arrears. Importantly, these no longer had to be paid before water could be turned back on. Suddenly the arguments about the prohibitive costs of providing the trickler system made in the Manqele case did not apply (*Post*, July 26, 2000). But mass mobilization continued. The council demanded that residents take personal responsibility for any tampering. On the day the Bayview Flat Residents' water case was to be heard, 200 people from Umlazi arrived at the High Court. Their water also had been cut. Their leaders had read about the Manqele and Bayview cases in the press and, as a result, they had come to protest in solidarity, whichever way the judgment went.

Even within their own logic of good governance, it is difficult to understand what the council thought they were doing by cutting off water. Biological necessity would sooner or later have sparked massive resistance to their policies. Neil Macleod, executive director of Durban Water Services, put up an affidavit in the Manqele case, which contends that 23,786 households have had their water cut off owing to non-payment during the first half of 2000. Working to a conservative ratio of four people per household, approximately 100,000 people are without any water at all. The actual figure is probably far higher.

It is also apparent from documents put up by the Metro Council in support of Macleod's affidavit, that the CCG's court action prevented a total of 20,955 disconnections scheduled for June 2000, the month in which the interdict was sought. During the same month, there were a corresponding number of only 6,111 reconnections.

If these figures are at all accurate, this means that for June 2000 alone the number of disconnections exceeded the number of reconnections by approximately 14,000. The number of 23,786 disconnected households was set to grow at an alarming rate. For the Durban Metro Council, the logic is that the only way to supply water services to the poor, who have no water services at present, is to deprive poor people who have water but are unable to pay for those services.

This revolving-sluice water provision policy is much the same as the Metro's revolving-door housing policy, where one group of poor people are evicted to make place, temporarily, for another. One gradually moves up the ubiquitous "waiting list," but through a process of displacement as much as through delivery. The policy, arguably, leaves city dwellers with pipes in their homes in a position worse than members of rural communities who have only a public standpipe or river some distance away. Living in a densely populated urban area, in an industrial basin heavily polluted by numerous factories, the residents of Umlazi and Chatsworth who have had their water cut off are suddenly without any access to drinkable water. In the cities, all taps have an owner and there is no public water supply within 50,500 or 5,000 meters of any house.

Currently, large sections of the townships in Durban are being pushed into the popular illegalities of clandestine water reconnections. And for various reasons, linked mainly to the short electoral cycles in this country, no ANC politician is likely to have the stomach for the "effective policing" that stopping these reconnections will require. In fact, it is doubtful that reconnections can be dealt with through the application of "criminal justice," even if the government was bold enough to try this route. What has been conspicuous by its absence from the council's response to the water crisis is the arrest on charges of malicious injury to property and/or theft, of even one individual for an unauthorized reconnection. There is no shortage of incidents or evidence of reconnections. Struggle plumbers abound. Indeed, when Manqele was argued, the Metro Council submitted videotapes to the court showing people, whom it identified, reconnecting water.

Instead the council's *modus operandi* is to send in small armies to re-disconnect, prompting, predictably, a dis-re-disconnection as soon as the troops leave. The Durban Metro is thus creating mass lawlessness by the sheer scale of its acts of oppression, which are bound to breed resistance. The cold doctrine that sees value in oppression, for the fight-back it generates, has, correctly, fallen into disrepute. However, it remains true that moving too soon against an adversary may spell doom. This has happened in Durban and nothing short of reconnecting all the water of those newly cut off and/or leaving those who have illegally reconnected alone, can stop some further confrontations developing. Water is essential for living, and no amount of exhortations to "revolutionary discipline" or *Masakhane* will stop those who cannot afford water from attempting to get it.

On August 21, 2000, the Bayview case was settled out of court. The applicants received a further concession. They did not have to pay the fixed water charge if they used more than six kiloliters, an amount equal to another ten kiloliters of water. Just how treacherous litigation in the bourgeois courts can be was revealed when Judge Jan Combrink was asked to make the settlement agreement an order of court. He was reluctant to do so stating that he would never have come to the assistance of the Bayview dwellers. What was all this crap about rights to water? He came from the Kalahari Desert. Indeed, the Metro Council's advocate's concessions were not legally necessary, but they were certainly politically necessary. Water court cases were becoming too much of a focal point for general disaffection and mobilization across the townships of Durban.

BEFORE I CEDE TOO MUCH CREDIT to the mobilization of the masses for the policy concessions that were made, it bears mention that local government elections were looming. By February 2001, when the case was heard in the Durban High Court, there was a less sympathetic response. The Durban High Court did not come to the aid of Thulisile Manqele, effectively ordering the disconnection of her water again.

The essence of Judge Vivien Niles-Duner's finding, handed down in February 2001, was that since regulations that have to be published in terms of the Water Services Act (and that would define "sufficient" water) have not been promulgated by the Water Ministry, Manqele has no enforceable rights in terms of that legislation.

It is not up to her, the judge said, to guess what the legislature or department have in mind. It may well be that the ministry has not published any regulations because they have made no budgetary provision to fund them.

The UniCity's advocate made much of the fact that Manqele had, probably, reconnected her water illegally in the past and thus could not be trusted not to tamper with any device installed to limit her water flow. As a result of her non-payment and her delinquent history, her water is to be disconnected as a "credit control" mechanism. The judge agreed.

One of the escape routes local government uses to evade its 2000 municipal election promises is the fact that people with historic rental, electricity, and water arrears are not entitled to the 6 kiloliter amount until they settle these arrears. Since the poor all have arrears that they cannot pay, they end up being excluded from the very policy that is meant to be for their benefit. On the other side of town, in the northern and western suburbs, the rich top up their swimming pools with the free 6 kiloliters.

Emboldened by the decision, the UniCity began sending out thousands of letters threatening disconnection. The person in charge of this initiative was named Mr. Stalin Joseph.

12. a revolt grows in isipingo

IN THE FLATS OF ISIPINGO, barely a stone's throw from Durban International Airport, people had taken heart from events in Chatsworth. Here too eviction notices had been received. Water and electricity cutoffs were already taking place.

A civic organization was already in place—the Isipingo Development Forum (IDF). Preggie Naidoo, a former teacher and union official in the South African Democratic Teachers Union (SADTU), a Congress of South African Trade Unions (COSATU) affiliate, started working in and revitalized this more or less dormant organization. Naidoo surrounded himself with a particularly strong "executive committee" that functioned formally, met regularly, and painstakingly took mandates from public meetings. Someone was authorized to make contact with the CCG.

On the other side of Isipingo's power divide was an illuminating combination of Democratic Alliance (DA) and ANC leaders, led by former apartheid-era mayor Pubal Naidoo and the incongruously named ANC councilors Happy Moodley and Tiger Pillay.

With the eviction dates looming, the first action was to confront the officials from the local municipality that had been sending out eviction notices. The municipal offices in Illovo were a forty-minute bus ride away. One day, two 70-seater busses and about 12 taxis arrived at these offices without warning. Tiger Pillay and Happy Moodley were summoned by the crowd. In no time, there was a massive police presence.

The stakes were high. The forthcoming election for places on the new Durban Unicity (an amalgamation of smaller municipalities in and around Durban) was to be held in December 2000, and was already on the horizon. With the crowd, again overwhelmingly female, threatening to storm the building, Tiger Pillay emerged into the foyer and announced to IDF and CCG leaders that the summonses would be withdrawn. Lured out of his offices with the promise that he could address the crowd and announce the concession as if it stemmed magnanimously from him, the microphone was

77

instead given to one resident after another, who heaped scorn upon Tiger Pillay. The understanding was that Pillay's speaking would defuse this vote-rich community's anger at the ANC. But this had been delightfully betrayed, and Pillay was left to complain bitterly to CCG leaders afterwards about his humiliation.

With the drive by local ANC and DA officials to "recover costs" from the poor of Isipingo set back, Pubal Naidoo decided to act. He went above the local municipality's head and wrote a letter to the ANC Head Office and to the mayor of Durban demanding that poor people in Isipingo (he called them "defaulters") be evicted. The gist of the letter asserted that they were criminals for not paying and for resisting eviction. He was later to deny he wrote the letter.

Pubal Naidoo belongs in a spaghetti western. A pastor in a charismatic Christian sect, former mayor, businessman, and local bigwig in the area, he had developed a fearful reputation for violence. With his telltale swag-ger, large gut, and booming voice, he knew how to get his way in the lit-tle town of Isipingo. His sons were his enforcers, keeping criticism of his controversial business dealings mute. One of his sons was a policeman at the local station, which seemed to give the whole family immunity from retribution.

At a huge mass meeting in the local town hall the contents of Naidoo's letter were made public. IDF chairperson Preggie Naidoo launched into a forthright attack on Pubal Naidoo saying things that ought to have been said a long time before. Pubal was a bully and a traitor to his people. He was also mortal. Seemingly buoyed by the fact that people from out of town like Orlean Naidoo from the Westcliff Flat Residents Association and other CCG fighters had joined them in the hall, it was unanimously decid-ed to march to Pubal Naidoo's house to confront him that very day. This was a major psychological advance for the community as Pubal had previ-ously been a law unto himself.

People streamed out of the hall and built up steam as they approached Pubal's gated mansion, some ten minutes' walk away. Pubal was not home. But his sons arrived. One of them, a policeman, pulled out his gun and waved it around wildly, threatening the crowd. The younger brother was sent to fetch more ammunition. Naidoo's daughter appeared on the bal-cony of his villa, hurling abuse at the crowd. A middle-aged lady yelled back, "I taught you when you were still in primary school. You had your head full of lice." The crowd took up the refrain, "Lice, lice, lice." Senorita

Naidoo dropped her jaw and fled inside the house in tears. Meanwhile the now crazed son swung his gun in all directions looking for a target for his anger and fear but the people refused to step back and stared him down.

It was a defining moment. Aunties, who had been cowed for years by the likes of Mayor Pubal, stood their ground. Groups of young men surged in and out of Pubal's property, on one occasion entering his house. Pubal later claimed some items had been broken, but others contested his claim. They were simply showing that he was not so untouchable after all. Finally, uniformed police arrived and young deputy sheriff Naidoo was disarmed. Pubal's neighbors all stood in the street, amazed, some gleeful, gawking at what was happening. The people's point had been made. They marched back to the hall. While residents of the flats still live in desperate and heartbreaking poverty, Pubal is no longer a factor in Isipingo politics. People now know what to do when eviction notices are served in Isipingo since the showdown at Pubal's villa. No one has been evicted since.

THIS WAS THE CONTEXT in which people in Isipingo and Chatsworth began to discuss the forthcoming UniCity elections of December 2000. Long debates were held within CCG ranks on the value of participating in some of the wards where the CCG had a presence. It was decided to support certain independent candidates and to allow the CCG to continue to mobilize outside the ambit of electoral politics.

Two constituencies were contested. In Chatsworth, the electoral area that encompassed the Westcliff Flats where the CCG had established a presence included large tracts of middle- class areas where the CCG had done no work. The other area was Isipingo. In Chatsworth the CCG made a strategic error in choosing its candidate. It decided to field Iqbal Sharma Meer, a person who was not resident in Chatsworth. A homegrown candidate in the form of the leader of the Westcliff Flat Residents Association, Orlean Naidoo, could not be convinced to stand. She still wanted to fight outside the system and was worried that people would see her past activism as being part of a plan for her to gain office.

In Isipingo, Preggie Naidoo stood as an independent candidate. His ward was geographically bigger, including areas where many African residents stayed. However, at a class level, things were more homogenous in his ward than the Chatsworth ward. The task facing CCG activists in both these areas was monumental—they had to work against the electoral machines and massive resources of the established political parties.

The campaign in Chatsworth was principled. "No to evictions, support for the illegal reconnections of water and electricity." There was no dragooning and ferrying of grannies and grandpas to the polling stations to vote for whom the grandkids had decided was best as occurred, particularly, in the Minority Front's campaign. The campaign was also stridently non-racial, not only in its publicity but also in its practice—African and Indian residents together were the campaign workers with no allowance made for the prejudices of voters who might want to be approached by campaigners of a particular race or religion. While this allowed the MF, none too subtly, to garner the conservative Indian vote, the campaign workers of the CCG were after more than votes. The struggle beyond the polling stations should not be compromised. And so when certain CCG stalwarts refused to vote at all because they believed no good would come of delegating people to sit on the UniCity Council, they were not prevailed upon to swallow their misgivings.

The MF's main candidate—the candidate it would have as UniCity mayor in the event of the MF gaining a majority—was deployed to stand in the Westcliff area. He appealed unashamedly to middle-class fears of the poor, with a bit of *swart gevaar* (black peril) thrown in, pointing to the dangers of the African squatter camps mushrooming inside Chatsworth. The DA was able to do the swart gevaar tactic better, but lost out to the MF on account of the Indian minority syndrome and ethnic chauvinism. The result was that the MF narrowly beat the DA in the ward that included the area of Westcliff/Bangladesh where the CCG had a stronghold. But while the CCG lost, it had by no means been routed. An analysis of these results in Chatsworth show that Meer was able to beat everybody in the voting station where the poors live, Bangladesh, hands down. Here Meer had over twice the votes of the DA and some three and a half times the vote of the MF.

In Isipingo, Preggie Naidoo, born and bred in the area and standing on the same ticket as Iqbal Meer, obtained a huge victory. In the whole of South Africa, he was the only independent candidate to win a seat in local government. The ward that included the Bayview Flatlands, Unit Two in Chatsworth, in which the CCG had decided to campaign for a no-vote, recorded voter turnout reminiscent of the days of the hated tricameral parliamentary system. In those days less than 15 percent of the electorate voted for a hated system; now, less than 20 percent of the registered voters cast their ballot. After the elections, mobilization to resist evictions continued, and drew in increasing numbers of people.

The ANC was only able to maintain the majority in the Unicity Executive Committee by signing a pact with the MF. KwaZulu Natal was a truly heterogeneous place politically speaking—the ANC dominated its big cities, the IFP controlled the provincial parliament, and just under half of those who could vote held their peace, not voting at all in its poorer areas.

The battle of Bayview:
security guards clash with
residents during evictions.

Temporary relief after the High
Court orders that the Durban
Council reconnects Thulisile
Manqele's water supply.
The decision was later reversed.

A struggle electrician in Soweto
illegally reconnects electricity cut
off by the major supplier, Eskom.

Ashraf Cassiem beaten by riot police during a protest against evictions
in Tafelsig, Cape Town

Joint protest of rabbis and Palestinian supporters at the World Conference
Against Racism in Durban

The Durban Social Forum march at the WCAR

Ashwin Desai addresses a meeting to protest water bills in Mpumalanga.

Mpumalanga protest march

Illegal squatters at Bredell, near Johannesburg, have their makeshift shelters destroyed.

13. mpumalanga's new war

IF YOU DROVE along the N3 highway between Durban and Johannesburg during the winter of 1987, about 30 kilometers out of Durban, just after passing by a road-sign that read Peacevale, you would see clouds of black smoke over the horizon on the left of the road. This smoke did not come from the annual sugarcane plantation burnings or a random veld fire. These were homes and cars and shops and people set alight in a mini civil war in the township just outside the industrial node of Hammarsdale. The protagonists were the comrades and "young lions" of the ANC fighting what they believed were the black stooges of the apartheid regime on the one side, and Inkatha Freedom Party war lords and their young *impis* defending the culture and sanctity of the Zulu nation from the godless, Xhosa-domi-nated communists of the liberation movements on the other hand.

If you were brave enough to go into Mpumalanga during the night, you would see almost no-one on the streets but would feel a thousand eyes peeping through curtains and windshields. Then suddenly the ominous thudding footfalls of one or other patrol of youths armed with Makarov and Tokarev handguns, AK47s, G3s, and police-issue Star 9mm pistols would be heard. There might be a clatter as the group ducked through backyards, jumped over fences and slunk between backyard shacks until they reached their destination. Then the flute-like clicks and grates of gun-metal before a fusillade of bullets were let fly. The shouting and wailing, the shrieking, would take a minute or so to begin. Lights would go on and perhaps a few optimistic shots would be fired in return. Not knowing whether the assassination had been accomplished or not, the attackers would light petrol bombs and lob these at flammable property in the vicin-ity. Inside blood would start flowing and children be gathered up in the arms of those not yet dead. Within five minutes the footfalls, much heavier and faster this time, would resume and make their demented way back up the road and away into the darkness and safety of home-turf. Occasionally one side would stage a provocative march through no man's land. During

these forays, those unlucky enough to be living in other areas would be
assaulted, chopped, or even killed. Mainly, however, daylight would bring
an eerie normality with people who had plotted each other's deaths the
night before boarding taxis to work together under the jaundiced gaze of
the security police and army. To analyse the so-called black-on-black violence in Mpumalanga is not the aim of this story. It happened, and it cost
hundreds of lives and caused untold misery and trauma over a period of
five years as ANC-aligned youth structures battled it out with the Inkatha
and KwaZulu government supported residents. I would like to tell you
about what peace brought.

MORE THAN FIVE YEARS after the adoption of the ANC's neoliberal economic plan, GEAR, the business node of Hammarsdale, just outside Durban, continues to exist. Barely. It appears suddenly at the end of a short
rural road just off the aforementioned N3 highway and consists of a grid of
streets forming 16 blocks. On each of these blocks, huge warehouses and
factories sit, ringed by serious fences. Half these factories will never
retrench again. They are already boarded up. Only a fraction of the people
who bravely boarded taxis to work during the violence are still required to
present themselves at factory gates. All the security guards at these gates
wear purple berets and are armed with shotguns with which they amble
around. Apart from two petrol stations, a funeral parlor, a take-out joint, a
branch of Pep Stores, and a dilapidated clothing union office, there is nothing else going on in the formal economy of Hammarsdale. Informally,
there is a market for fruit and traditional remedies adjacent to the taxi
rank. Ultra-informally, there are grandparents' pensions, stock theft, pilfer-
ing, and prostitution at the Freeway Truck Stops.

Hammarsdale has never been lived in. All the houses and shacks are to
be found five kilometers further inland, in a township once renowned for
its violence called Mpumalanga. This township provided the labor power for
Hammarsdale textile factories at much lower rates than Durban while
employers capitalized on all kinds of incentives provided by the apartheid
state to bring industries to the "border areas" of the former homelands. The
legacy of the violent clashes of the previous decade can still be seen in the
burnt-out houses and cars and areas that remain more or less no-go areas
for the ANC or the IFP. Peace was made but the divisions and distrust
remain. Reflecting on those times, Sipho Mlaba, a community leader and
former IFP strongman, says that walking in Unit 3, an ANC hub, would have

meant certain death for him. The same applies in reverse for Maxwell Cele, a former ANC activist, should he have set foot in the IFP- controlled Unit 1.

Since 1994 the old wounds have been healed between these men and those who look up to them as leaders. Mpumalanga has been praised as a model of reconciliation with Sipho Mlaba receiving the Martin Luther King Prize for Peace. Nowadays, he and Maxwell Cele move everywhere together. They are comrades but the peace they have achieved is gone. Once again there are rows of armored personnel carriers patrolling Mpumalanga. Military patrols move through the streets swaying their assault rifles from side to side, looking tensely over their shoulders. Every so often teargas and birdshot are fired at residents and the youth set fire to barricades. The SABC radio still refers to residents "running amok" and politicians still talk about "agitators" and threaten "clampdowns." This time the residents of Mpumalanga are not fighting for or against "national liberation" or "Zulu self-determination," the battle cries of the 1980s. They are united in resisting the neoliberal policies of the ANC–dominated local government elected for the Durban Unicity in 2000 as well as the IFP controlled government of the KwaZulu-Natal province. Many people, both inside and outside Mpumalanga comment on this startling political realignment and are unable to explain why such a high level of militance exists in this particular township around social issues when locations all over South Africa are suffering the grinding effects of the new government's economic policies also.

MPUMALANGA HAS A PECULIAR HISTORY, and this history does much to explain its unusual capacity for solidarity and resistance. Since an African landholding class emerged there in the mid-19th century, on land bought by the Methodist Church to establish a mission station, it has defied the patterns of South African history. In most of Natal colonial officials were often able to install corrupt or pliant chiefs and use them to ensure that white settlers could get access to land and labor on their own terms. But in Mpumalanga a well-developed and independent-minded black middle class was able to provide leadership when tribal chiefs did not, and preserve a remarkable measure of self-government.

This endured until the 1960s when the apartheid government made a concerted effort to break this independence. In 1961 the area was declared a decentralization point to encourage businesses (mainly foreign) to invest in Bantustan areas. Almost immediately after the declaration, the government expropriated land to establish a township for workers at the new factories. The African landholding class was weakened, but owners and tenants with nowhere else to go—mainly women—fought back against eviction with remarkable success considering the complete crushing of similar campaigns in Sophiatown and District Six. With new job- seekers flooding into the area, and squatter settlements constantly expanding, it was only in the mid-1970s that a stable local authority could be established. This was essential from the point of view of the Nationalist parties efforts to disguise the hideousness of apartheid behind the lie that Black self-government was taking place in separate tribal areas. The township manager appointed by the government and township council intended to oversee Mpumalanga's incorporation into the homeland of the kwaZulu began by raising rents and forcing people to get rid of their livestock; the latter being an extremely traumatic event vividly recalled by almost every man or woman old enough to remember it.

Having resisted the worst depredations of colonial rule and apartheid social engineering, Mpumalanga also resisted the authority of Inkatha, the ruling party in the kwaZulu homeland that used its control over social services and employment to entrench its domination. The business community, mainly small traders, gave their support to the Mpumalanga Residents Association (MPURA) that captured control of the township council in 1981. The Mpumalanga election was one of only a handful of elections where the outcome was not a foregone conclusion and a real contestation of power occurred. Ironically, formal incorporation into kwaZulu had provided Mpumalangans with what many other Black South Africans did not have, a semblance of a vote in a situation where the apartheid state and its local functionaries could be challenged through the ballot box. The Azanian Peoples Organization (AZAPO)—inspired by the ideology of black consciousness and opposed to any participation in the homeland system—secured a foothold in Mpumalanga before being forced to flee the area by Inkatha vigilantes in about 1982. But as countrywide resistance to apartheid grew, Inkatha dominance was challenged this time by the ANC–aligned Hammarsdale Youth Congress (HAYCO), which had emerged in 1986 and was a reflection of radical youth formations springing up all over the country. Violent conflicts between Inkatha and Hayco continued. People in civil war situations, talk about a spiral of violence. So compulsive did the blood-letting become that when Vusi Maduna, the charismatic president of HAYCO, presented his comrades with a cease-fire proposal he had negotiated with the IFP, they turned on him with accusations of being a spy and he was shot (*City Press*, March 22, 1987). Finally, after persistent efforts by Sipho Mlaba, a peace agreement was brokered in 1989 but violence flared up again after the release of Nelson Mandela in 1990. This antagonism would firstly be channeled into warring electoral machines and the flow of blood finally plugged with a truce in which provincial power was ceded to the IFP and national power to a government of national unity lead by the ANC in 1994.

Every time one moves around the township, one cannot avoid the question of what allows the slightly crazed guy at the taxi rank, who drags his left leg behind him, where a Hayco comrade severed his ligaments with a panga, to march together with this same comrade against the ANC UniCity council? What allows Mandla Gwala, staunch adherent of the Black Consciousness philosophy that eschewed any contamination with the IFP, to organize together with IFP warlords of yore?

AFTER THE ELECTIONS IN 2000, and in line with the new city demarcations, the Durban Unicity Council started to try to assert control over the township that had successfully warded off the attentions of Ulundi and Pretoria during the apartheid era. It did this not in the name of party political power but out of a commitment to neoliberal budgetary policies. In Mpumalanga no water meters existed and people paid a flat rate of R10 per month for this service. This would do the profiteers in the UniCity no good and the order was given to begin installing these devices. In addition the UniCity demanded extravagant payment that inflated people's bills for lights and rates from R26 a month to over R200. Considering the statistics garnered by the University of Natal's Institute for Black Research that some 3,500 residents of Mpumalanga who had found work in Hammarsdale had lost their jobs during the period 1998–2001 as well as their calculation that the average per capita income per month of people living in Unit 1 is a mere R23.70, the UniCity demands seem, as the saying goes, like trying to squeeze blood from a stone. As one resident put it, "This ANC don't know that apartheid left us with nothing. And now they want something from nothing".

The spark that started the fierce Mpumalanga mobilization against the UniCity in 1999 was the arrival in the township of squads of UniCity laborers and plumbers with trucks full of water meters and PVC piping. Until then, Mpumalanga residents paid (or didn't pay if they had no money) a flat rate for the water they received. Now the Durban UniCity set about trying to attach water meters to each private erf as well as to public (but now pay-as-you-go) standpipes. The people of Mpumulanga immediately knew what this meant. When electricity meters were installed as part of the grand *Masakhane* fanfare in 1997, few people could afford the bills, particularly during the brisk Midland winter. Sipho Mlaba maintains that there was a direct increase in crime after electricity meters were installed, with the unemployed having to steal for the cash needed to buy energy.

Indeed, it was an incident of shoplifting at Mlaba's spaza shop that prompted his own remarkable conversion from Durban Metro Councilor to community activist and intractable foe of his former colleagues. Mlaba was furious when he caught seven-year-old Sipho trying to leave the spaza shop he owns with a half kilogram of sugar beans without paying. Where was this child's mother while he was out stealing? Mlaba walked with the child in one hand and the beans in the other to the shack where Sipho's mother lived. She was sleeping. Mlaba insisted that she wake-up and explain why she was neglecting her thieving child. Her reply jolted him: "Baba Mlaba, I was so hungry and there is no food, so I just decided to sleep."

After surveying the bare hovel, Mlaba left both Sipho and the beans in the shack and went back to his shop depressed and embarrassed. It was at about this time that the City Council agreed to pay the newly privatized Umgeni Water provider's price hikes and to recover their cost of supplying water to the township of Mpumalanga (as well as making a tidy profit above that). For this to occur, water meters would need to be installed. In response to these plans, the people at first sent delegates to ask for assurances that the indigent would be exempt from having to pay. According to Maxwell Cele, they were laughed at in city hall. Community members were told what the deal was: contractors would be coming to install water meters and every woman, man, child, and animal in Mpumalanga would, from that day on, be treated as a customer. There would be no exceptions.

The Mpumalanga community reacted with a vengeance, ripping up the meters and chasing contractors away. Running battles were fought with police. By the third day, the biscuit- colored gadgets used to attach the water meters lay strewn throughout the township. Mlaba himself tried to intervene in a tense stand-off between three or four thousand angry residents and a line of police. In the melee he was bitten by a police-dog and the woman standing next to him was tear gassed and beaten so badly that she has now lost her sight. When things had calmed down, Mlaba told a newspaper reporter that he supported what the people were doing as they had no money to pay. His comments made headlines everywhere. Since he was a city councilor at the time, Mlaba was hauled before a disciplinary meeting where he was required to sign a code of conduct outlawing any statement that went against council policy. To his eternal credit, Mlaba resigned rather than sign.

Maxwell Cele has a history of coal-face struggle that was earned during the days that SACP stalwart Harry Gwala still stomped about the Natal Midlands. He took the initiative of meeting with his old foe Mlaba during the first round of water meter protests in 2000 and suggested that they work together. Harried out of the ANC for this decision, he denies that he is a new kind of community leader: "No one is in charge of the protests, except the anger and hunger in every person."

Before long, the council stopped sending in contractors. Things returned to normal. No water meters were installed. Cele ascribes the backing-off of the ANC dominated council to "electioneering." "We were still 'comrades' before December 5 [the date of municipal elections], but now we are consumers again."

In 2001 the new UniCity Council intensified the installation of water meters. Again residents resisted with intent, ripping up the water meters. Ten thousand people attended rallies, the speeches were hot and the demands steadfast—free essential services for the poor. Beautifully, the brave, responsible, physically capable youth of the Inkatha Youth Brigade and the hip, intellectual and earnest youngsters from a Congress tradition reached out to each other during these times. New alliances and loyalties were being formed in the adrenaline of this uprising. But the repression was also harsher than ever. The army was called in and meetings were "banned." The superintendent of the Mpumalanga police-station tells of frantic calls by city councilors to ensure that the local stadium is blocked off as a meeting point. Some people were arrested for breaking meters and charged with this crime. Mlaba and Cele have been deemed worthy of personal attack, being branded "counter-revolutionaries." Cele laughs. "Everybody in Mpumalanga can see, the real counter-revolutionaries are in this government."

In May 2001 a mass meeting was held outside an empty but heavily-guarded stadium to protest the installation of water meters. It was called by CCF affiliate, the Mpumalanga Concerned Group. The meeting was, however, unlike all other protests in Mpumalanga. Professor Fatima Meer from the CCF was there and she gave a rousing speech. Also on the platform were activists from the Soweto Electricity Crisis Committee and community leaders from Umlazi. The large army and police presence did not deter speakers from making forthright statements. They viewed the continual demand for payment for every bit of dignity and citizenship they received to be an attack on them, the poor. They would respond in kind. This response, Professor Meer said, would no longer be an isolated Mpumalanga or Chatsworth matter but something concerning the poor across the province and country. Her words proved to be prophetic.

However, the arrest of water-meter saboteurs took its toll. Maxwell Cele's Toyota, used to ferry people to and fro on CCF business, was impounded. With the army on constant patrol there was also the danger that activists could be shot during their nightly escapades. Indeed, two people loosely associated with the Mpumalanga Concerned Group were shot dead, allegedly for being "criminals," by a shadowy vigilante group operating out of a still tightly controlled ANC unit. When former Mpumalanga resident and now ANC bigwig, Meshack Radebe, started making statements in support of rooting out "criminals" in Mpumalanga, it seemed to many that open season had been declared on the activists too. Shortly thereafter, Council workers were replaced with hired hands from the community, a clever move by the UniCity providing fertile ground for further intra-community conflict between people desperate for piece-work and the Mpumalanga Concerned Group. It seemed conditions were being created for a resumption of the horrendous violence that had scarred this place before. Some in the Mpumalanga Concerned Group advocated meeting fire with fire. After all, they retained a residual capacity to, shall we say, defend themselves fairly effectively. But others argued that violence would only play into the new enemy's hands. And so, after a late night meeting at which these developments were discussed, it was decided to abandon the physical opposition to the installation of water meters but to continue insisting that, no matter what these meters recorded in the future, the genuinely indigent would not have their supply disconnected for not paying their bills.

The result of calling off the sabotage policy was that whomever had counted on profiting from an eruption of violence was denied this opportunity. For four or five months, the Mpumalanga Concerned Group went into a sort of hibernation waiting for that fateful day when the conditions for maximum unity amongst all in the township would again arise—when the first bills were pushed under people's doors. And sure enough, in early February 2002, residents from all units both ANC and IFP and even those individuals who had dug the holes and installed water meters themselves,

received stern letters threatening imminent disconnection should outstanding accounts not be paid immediately.

These amounts ranged from between R600 to R1200 and this for four
months' consumption. Apparently the City Council also added previous
electricity arrears to the bills. Since most of those who had received electricity in 1997 had already been disconnected for not being able to afford
payment, the UniCity had not had real leverage to get these outstanding
amounts debts liquidated. However, now they had such leverage: the disconnection of the absolute necessity of water. This consolidation of
accounts further added to the amounts owed so that some residents found
themselves R10,000 or more in arrears.

In March 2002, in the full yet magnanimous glow of vindication, the
Mpumalanga Concerned Group called a mass march to the local rent office.
Schools were closed for the day, taxi ranks did not operate, roads were sealed
off, and churchmen gave the event their blessing. Police estimates were that
ten thousand people took part. I am bad with numbers but it looked bigger
than that with the throng stretching three kilometers into the distance. On
arrival at the rent office, the masses did not burn their water accounts as I
had expected. Nor did they hurl abuse at the police or storm the building.
Some holding a single green note and other rubbing two coins together
were demanding to pay R10 for their monthly services and no more. To see a
massive crowd all baying to pay, but to pay what they could afford, was both
amazing and slightly disconcerting. The television people who were there
too, also struggled to conceal their amazement, amusement, and respect for
this demand. The coverage the march got on prime time television was wonderful. Imagine groups of 50 people pushing against the heavy wire gates of
the Rent Office and then being let in, in a great rush to pay. Imagine UniCity
officials obliged to receive and process each singular payment. Imagine the
sense of having discharged one's "legitimate" obligations to the government
after having paid up. Imagine, all the while this is going on, songs being
sung and speeches being given, ridiculing the president, the mayor, and the
local councilors, threatening to sweep them all from power with ten rand
marches like this throughout the country.

And sure enough, soon the idea took off in Tafelsig in Cape Town, where
residents put together their own ten rand march on March 28, 2002. As I
write, another ten rand march is being organized in Durban, that will
involve Chatsworth, Wentworth, Umlazi, and Mpumalanga.

14. fighting neoliberalism in Soweto and tafelsig

> We don't ask why or when people are cut off, we just switch
> them back on. Everyone should have electricity.

—VIRGINIA SETSHEDI, Soweto Electricity Crisis Committee,
November 2001

> It does not matter whether the Democratic Alliance or the
> ANC rules Cape Town. Both will disconnect our water and evict us
> because both have a policy of privatization and neoliberalism.

—Speaker at an anti-eviction rally, Cape Town, January 2002

IT WAS NOT ONLY IN DURBAN that resistance to the new government and its policies was being bred. Struggles led by independent community-based organizations flared up all over South Africa. Those closer to the action in Soweto in Gauteng and Tafelsig in the Western Cape are better able to make sense of the dramatic developments in these areas. But in the townships of Durban, Cape Town, and Johannesburg the issues were the same: cost recovery was causing government to attack its own citizens in ways reminiscent of the apartheid days.

Trevor Ngwane, a resident and activist from Pimville in Soweto, was one of those who thought that the ANC would be able to address the concerns of the poor by dealing with high service charges, high rents, and the lack of facilities. Deeply rooted in the community, he was elected as a councilor in 1995, representing the ANC. When Walter Sisulu was released from prison and went back to Soweto, he had said, "Much of Soweto has not changed since I first came to live here in the thirties . . . With few exceptions the matchbox houses are very much the same. A government who is not addressing the basic issue of decent housing is not seriously committed towards political change."[1]

Implicit in Sisulu's statement was that conditions in Soweto were going to improve once the ANC assumed power. But the reality was that, for many, things were going to get worse and more difficult. The ANC–dominated Johannesburg council, elected in 1995, planned to privatize as many of the council's services as possible. This would not only lead to retrenchment of workers but would rapidly hike the price of services and cause a clampdown of unimaginable proportions on those who were too poor to pay for the meager services they were receiving. Trevor Ngwane, newly elected to that council, knew that the logic of cost recovery would not aid his constituency in Soweto and would only serve to deepen their misery. He raised his voice in opposition. He was suspended from the ANC and then expelled.

Trevor Ngwane joined with activists like Virginia Setshedi and Dudu Mphenyeke and began to organize against these policies through an organization called the Soweto Electricity Crisis Committee (SECC).

Residents of Soweto were faced with a concerted policy of electricity cutoffs after the 1999 general election was won by the ANC, who had promised the exact opposite. Some twenty thousand houses had their electricity supplies disconnected every month. (*Mail and Guardian*, June 8, 2001). Brian Johnson, the manager of Eskom indicated that "the aim is to disconnect at least 75 percent of Soweto residents" (*Mail and Guardian*, April 6, 2001). The SECC found that most residents in the townships who manage to find work earn less than R800 a month; almost half the households surveyed survived on an old-age pension of R540 a month. Unemployment was spiraling, with some areas of Soweto reaching 80 percent. Despite the poverty and hardship the SECC found that Eskom had an unfair and discriminatory tariff system. As Ngwane was to expose to the media, "people in Soweto are paying more for electricity than the people of the Beverly Hills–like suburb of Sandton." In Soweto, the cost of electricity is 28 cents a kilowatt a unit, in Sandton it's 16 cents, big business gets charged 7 cents, and the worst-off, in the rural areas, pay 48 cents" (*Mail and Guardian*, April 6, 2001).

The SECC mobilized against the cutoffs. They launched Operation Khanyisa, meaning "to light." This campaign meant the deliberate flouting of legality with the reconnection of electricity to households in Soweto. Sifiso Sithole is one of the reconnectors. He is 16 years old and goes to a local high school. He lives with his ailing grandmother who owes R10,000 to Eskom. On a documentary aired on South African television on November 13, 2000, Sifiso brazenly showed off his skills as a reconnecter, lighting up the life of Eunice Zwane, a pensioner. According to Virginia Setshedi the SECC gets about fifty calls a day from the community. "We don't ask why or when people were cut off, we just switch them back on. Everyone should have electricity" (Washington Post, November 6, 2001).

On June 6, 2001, the Sowetans marched on the Moroka Police Station to protest against the high handedness of Eskom security guards who were assaulting and bullying members of the community. Eskom security guards arrived at the scene and opened fire, shooting three protestors.

Angered residents decided to march on the house of Johannesburg Mayor, Amos Masondo on June 9, 2001. From all corners of Soweto residents marched to Umfulo North. From there they marched for two and a half hours to Jabulani Southern Metropolitan Substructure. All along the way they chanted revolutionary songs with the favorite calling Mbeki "a black dog." The mayor was not there to receive the memorandum. The memorandum from the SECC demanded:

1   An immediate moratorium on electricity cutoffs.
2   Scrap all arrears.
3   Stop estimates. Cut unemployment by employing people to read meters every month so that all bills reflect annual consumption.
4   No charges for reconnection.
5   Implement the promise for free electricity now! We demand a free lifeline supply of at least 200 kwh per person per day.
6   End the subsidies from the poor to the rich. A new block tariff system that is equitable, affordable and based on the principle that the rich must subsidize the poor, with charges increasing with consumption above the free-lifeline level.
7   Stop the privatization of Eskom.
8   No discrimination against informal settlements. Electricity for all.
9   All councilors must pledge their support for these demands or resign and make way for representatives who are prepared to stand by their communities or be recalled immediately.

It concluded: "If our demands are not met we will have no alternative but to embark on a campaign of mass non-payment."

The activities of the SECC and the airing of a sympathetic documentary on national television led to an angry response from the government. Minister of Public Enterprises Jeff Hadebe compared the SECC to a "gang of criminals" and promised to hunt down those who could not pay and had to resort to illegal connections (*Sunday Times*, December 12, 2001). The newly formed National Anti-Privatisation Forum Co-ordinating Committee (NAPFCC), which includes the SECC, responded with equal virulence: "The NAPFCC considers such talk to be disrespectful of the very people who fought the racist apartheid government to put Radebe and his cohorts where they are today: in the lap of luxury while the poor continue to suffer miserably . . . The NAPFCC will not allow the ANC's privatization of essential services such as water, electricity, housing, education, and health to turn us, the poor and working class, into criminals, while a small group of corrupt politicians have chosen to spend money we need for basic services and jobs on a worthless arms deal."

The SECC received invaluable support from progressive NGOs in the city, like the Alternative Information and Development Center (AIDC) and the Municipal Services Project. Activists have jobs here and their facilities are made available for mobilization work. However questions remain about how funding and other opportunities that are obtained in the name of these struggles are disbursed. A tendency to capitalize on the research, publication, and conference opportunities created for those associated with these struggles is causing some unhappiness among people actually involved in the grassroots organizations. There is always an opening for academics to focus only on those parts of the politics of which they personally approve and to caricature more militant strategies.

Despite these dangers, an umbrella body, the Anti-Privatization Forum, brings together these same free-floating intellectuals, the SECC militants, radical student types, the Landless People's Movement, and a range of smaller issue-based left groups. Watchful, networked, and committed, they are able to respond collectively and coherently to global events from this organizational vantage point.

IF YOU DRIVE AWAY from the mountain in Cape Town, along the national highway the N2, you will pass the turnoff into Mitchell's Plain, the notoriously bleak township where the apartheid regime dumped "colored" people. Turning into Mitchell's Plain, following the main road till it pushes against the dunes that signal the end of available space, you'll find Tafelsig—a mass of council houses and sandy streets that has a reputation, even in Mitchell's Plain, for gangsterism and poverty.

The tar on the main road is still warped by the heat of the burning barricades that residents erected during the recent anti-eviction revolt. The events that triggered the formation of the Tafelsig Anti-Eviction Campaign invaded bourgeois Cape Town via the front page of the *Cape Times*: a picture of Ashraf Cassiem lying on the ground, a police boot frozen in mid-swing, aimed at his head.

That morning, October 17, 2000, the police came to evict the family of Charles Lategan, in Olifantshoek Road, Tafelsig. This was not the first time that the Lategan family had been evicted: the sheriff had come before, but each time the family was removed from their house, members of the local community simply broke the locks off the doors and moved them back in. So this time the sheriff was backed up with force. Again, the community reacted—a crowd of people stood outside the Lategan house, arguing with the police. Ashraf was prominent amongst them—a loudmouth, in police terms—arguing about constitutional rights, and so on. For that he was targeted, knocked to the ground, and beaten. His mother, Siyaam Cassiem, saw this from her second-story window, and rushed down to confront the police, and was in turn assaulted. Horribly. Siyaam Cassiem is on a disability grant—she has a weak heart. As she fell on top of her son, she suffered a heart attack.

In the aftermath of the eviction of the Lategans, and the assaults on the Cassiem family and others, a group of people in Tafelsig decided to form an Anti-Eviction Campaign. Up until that point the municipal policy on evictions had been haphazard—from time to time eviction notices were issued, and sheriffs moved in, but their actions were easily reversed. The use of large numbers of police, however, signaled the beginning of a new phase of struggle, and an interim committee of six decided to form a campaign to address the community's problems. The events in Olifantshoek Road also attracted the attention of activists from outside the area—and thus the campaign started: community activists from Tafelsig supported by resources donated by outside activists started taking stock of their situation. The first action undertaken was a comprehensive survey of households to try to ascertain the extent of the problem. From that door-to-door work grew the launch of the campaign in February 2001.

On February 18, 2001, the hall of the Tafelsig Community Center was packed to capacity—an estimated 500 people were present for the launch of the Tafelsig Anti-Eviction Campaign. Also present were people from other "colored" areas, who were facing similar problems.

The Cape Town UniCity Council (formed by the amalgamation of all municipalities in the greater Cape Town area in late 2000) had inherited a stock of council housing from the apartheid regime, council housing that was only made available for "colored" communities (since "Africans" were not meant to settle permanently in Cape Town). In terms of the neoliberal vision that the UniCity was pursuing, this housing was a source of nothing but problems and debt. Council houses in Cape Town have typically not been maintained for over twenty years, and the rent collected over time is often worth more than the value of the houses. Yet in the UniCity's terms, the problem lies entirely with the tenants—a history of massive unemployment has left many tenants in arrears, and as the mayor's spokesperson has said, the UniCity wishes to pursue an aggressive "credit control" policy.

This policy has had many names, but probably the most ironic is the "pro-poor" policy. Where previously households that could prove that they were indigent had certain service charges reduced or scrapped, the neoliberal-inspired "pro-poor" policy combined a set of "affordable" payment rates (often demanding hundreds of rands in down payments) with harsh penalties should payments be missed.

The emergence of a mass-based campaign of protest in Tafelsig, and the newly formed UniCity's insistence on resolving the municipal legacy of apartheid along neoliberal lines, resulted in a standoff. The UniCity flooded Tafelsig with "pink papers," final notices that action was going to be taken against Tafelsig residents. In response, the Anti-Eviction Campaign organized a "pink paper day"—everyone who received a pink paper pinned it to their chest, like a ribbon, and marched down to the rent office.

The strength of the Anti-Eviction Campaign was that it was rooted in the day-to-day operation of Tafelsig as a community. A woman said at the launch of the campaign, "We're not just fighting for houses, we're fighting to build the community." The surveys undertaken by the Anti-Eviction Campaign revealed that 70 percent of adults in Tafelsig are unemployed. It is common for three generations of a family—grandparents, parents, and children—to share a council house, and live off a single pension or disability grant. The poor condition of the houses means that health problems are common. The prospect of starvation is present every day. Many households don't have enough money for food—one household surveyed by the campaign had not eaten anything solid for two weeks.

In the context of the relentless poverty in Tafelsig, the role women play in building structures of communal responsibility has become a vital part of day-to-day existence. The meeting that launched the campaign was mostly comprised of women, and in the crowds that confront sheriffs and police, women are always prominent.

When the word spread that people were fighting evictions in Tafelsig, people from all over Cape Town started to phone the Tafelsig organizers. Already, at the founding meeting of the campaign, there had been speakers from Valhalla Park and Lavender Hill—now groups from Delft, Elsies River and elsewhere started making contact. In all these areas, a hidden struggle had been going on. Everywhere the pattern was the same—groups of residents, with no money and few resources, were fighting the council's crackdown on the poor. From all these struggles, the Western Cape Anti-Eviction Campaign was born.

The Western Cape campaign played a pivotal role mobilizing people across the Cape Peninsula, and linking together these geographically divided struggles. One of the first actions of the campaign was to organize a mass march on the mayor's office in Cape Town—despite the difficulties in getting money for buses. Some one thousand people marched down Adderley Street, chanting "Julle sit die mense uit, ons sit die mense in. Julle sit die water af, ons sit die water aan" (You throw the people out, we put them back in. You cut the water off, we put it back on).

On the march, the largely "colored" communities that formed part of the campaign were joined by residents from the "African" townships, KTC, Gugulethu, and Khayelitsha. In those areas, where people were still forced to live in shacks, the council had also been taking action—cutting off water and seizing the assets of the poorest of the poor. Outside Mayor Peter Marais' office, confronted by a wall of riot police, the poor of Cape Town sat discussing whether to try to break their way in. Eventually, however, Marais agreed to come out, but only if surrounded by riot police, and given the opportunity to speak from a police armored vehicle. This he did, to a combination of applause and derision, offering to consider the marchers' demands. That was the last anyone heard from Marais. The memorandum given to the council was never answered.

Since then, the Tafelsig organization has had to confront periodic attacks on this or that household by the authorities. Much like the organization in Chatsworth, it has become amoeba- like. When there's a need for action it expands and increases in density. In between, it shrinks, concerning itself mainly with resolving community disputes and providing a kind of social worker service to the many broken people living there. Ishmael Peterson and Hassim Jacobs are the mainstays of the Anti-Eviction Campaign in Tafelsig during these times, helping people process disability grant applications, giving legal advice, always, always sorting out problems.

When water-cut-offs hit Mitchell's Plain, these activists commissioned a fascinating piece of precision engineering at a nearby bush mechanic's shop. Numerous 30 centimeter pipes were tooled with screw threads on either side, which, with minor adjustments, could be inserted into the portion of the water meter that council officials had removed, thus restarting the stopped water supply. It can just as effortlessly be removed in a hurry.

Peterson and Jacobs have forged strong links with the neighboring, mainly African residents of Lost City and Silver City, who stay in recently built and already falling-apart starter homes. But activism still has its price in South Africa. They have warded off attempts on their lives and, in Peterson's case, his conscience after the local ANC parliamentary office offered him a well-paying full-time job in exchange for his leaving community politics.

IN THE ABSENCE OF DIALOGUE with the council, the campaign was organized along other lines. Looking outside Cape Town, the campaign developed links with the struggles against eviction and service disconnections that were going on in Durban—e-mails were printed out and circulated, news of the Durban successes spread by word of mouth. These contacts helped to dispense with one myth that bedeviled the Cape Town campaign—the myth that action against the poor was purely a policy of the Democratic Alliance (DA). The Western Cape was at that time the one province in South Africa governed by the DA—an alliance of the two major parties that had dominated the whites-only parliament, and the DA also controlled the UniCity council.

In the "colored" areas of Cape Town, the rivalry between the DA and the ANC was intense, with each making extravagant promises at election time, in a bid to secure the all-important "colored" vote. From the launch of the campaign in Tafelsig, organizers insisted on their independence from political parties, knowing that fighting over party allegiance was a potent dividing force. The news from Durban provided vital evidence that the war on the poor was not a party affair, but was waged equally by the ANC in Durban and the DA in Cape Town.

The Anti-Eviction Campaign has not, thus far, been able to stop this war, but the cost to the council of waging it has been dramatically increased. The initiative of poor communities in self- organizing, re-housing evicted families, and re-connecting disconnected water supplies (often using inventive local technology), and the courage of campaigners to fight the police in the streets, has meant that to enforce the war on the poor in Cape Town is now no simple thing.

When action needs to be taken by the council, it can only be taken at the cost of deploying hundreds of police and militarizing entire neighborhoods, an operation that cannot be sustained for more than a few days at a time. This was the case with the evictions in Tafelsig in May, and the water disconnections in September. By and large, the actions of the council grind to a halt—the poor of Cape Town will not simply die quietly, and the campaign is growing, both in numbers and in ability. Despite a recent spate of violent cutoffs by a rampant provincial government, with the DA having split and the Western Cape's murky politics now being lead by an alliance between the ANC and the New National Party, the Anti-Eviction Campaign in Cape Town is a sign of a new stage in struggle, a stage that won't be over soon.

1   Anthony Sampson, *Mandela: The Authorised Biography* (London, HarperCollins, 1999), p. 396.

15. labor and community: the volkswagen and engen strikes

The workers who went on strike were a mixed bag, they were
essentially old-guard unionists-many long-serving members
at the plant, nearing retirement—who were seen
as ideologically faithful to the old school of thinking where
managements are the enemy.

—MTUTUZELI TOM, president of NUMSA

To all NUMSA members we say: don't allow the leadership
to victimize the fighter at VWSA—today it is us, tomorrow
it will be you! To all COSATU members, an injury to one is an injury
to all! To the VW workers across the world, we together produce
the wealth of the company—let us stand together—today it is us,
tomorrow who knows who will be next? To all workers
everywhere, we need your support now!

—WILFUS NDANDANI, chairperson of the VWSA strike committee

GIVEN THE SCALE OF THEIR CONTRIBUTION to the struggle against
apartheid, one would expect the unions to lead the fight for social justice
in the new South Africa. This is not the reality, however. As the story of the
strike at Volkswagen shows, the big trade unions are part of the bulwark
that is preventing autonomous and radical resistance developing against
the ANC and its neoliberal policies.

The stage was set for the strike when VW, sensing the government's commitment to liberalizing the economy and the offer of attractive incentives
for exports, started to make substantial new investments in their plant at
Uitenhage near Port Elizabeth. German management replaced locals, technology was upgraded and there was a possibility of a huge export order in

the form of the production of 68,000 Golf motorcars. VW was also encouraged by the ability of both NUMSA national and the local shop stewards to
police agreements. This was important because VW was demanding certain
concessions from the union before it consolidated its investment. These
involved the key issue of "flexibility" to ensure the ability to "remain competitive in the global economy." VW wanted the union to agree to:

—a continuous production schedule based on a work week spread
over six days with a rotating day off;
—no overtime pay for weekend work;
—compulsory overtime without advance notice;
—overtime up to two 12-hour shifts and 70-hour weeks;
—the reduction of tea breaks from two to one per shift;
—the restructuring of annual holidays from the traditional three-
week Christmas–New Year shutdown to an individualized vacation
schedule for each worker;
—the elimination of washing-up time on the clock;
—the introduction of a pass system to control workers' movement
from one part of the plant to another;
—changes in the employer-funded pension that cost the workers 17
percent in new interest charges.[1]

Shockingly, the worker representatives signed the deal. According to Binisle
Mzeku, a worker who later went on strike against his own union for signing
this deal, "the NUMSA trade union secretaries had talks and concluded an
agreement on working practices with the VW management without listening to the opinions of the workers and local shop stewards." The agreement
involved a whole range of worsened conditions that were apparently agreed
to in order to increase the competitiveness of VW in South Africa.

    In fact, says Mzeku, taken as a whole, working conditions are worse now
than they were under the apartheid regime. Workers, he said, "learnt
about the signing in the newspaper." The shop stewards were younger
workers who had assumed office in 1996 and who seemed to be quite
bedazzled by the perks this brought. The older union representatives had
stepped aside hoping the new faces would bring new energy to the union.
But there was increasing discontent in the plant as the workers felt that
the shop stewards and the union head office seemed determined to steam-
roll changes demanded by management.

Mzeku's assessment was that "improvements which workers had gradually won in the apartheid period were taken back." These gains had been won in bloody battles with management. In one four-month period in 1989 there were thirty industrial actions at VWSA. These included nine strikes and fifteen work stoppages. Bit by bit, the management had conceded decent conditions. But now, management was using every opportunity to roll back the gains of the 1980s.

With no general meetings called, the older workers started to call lunchtime meetings. The "new" old leadership became known as *indlu ye ngwevu*, the "house of senators," and was semi-clandestine in operation. In 1999 they made a play for power. The NUMSA bureaucracy openly opposed them. But thirteen of them were elected shop stewards. The union's approach was to seek to expel them. According to the NUMSA president Mtutuzeli Tom: "They needed to be expelled as they went against union policy and they were undisciplined." Workers refused to have the shop stewards replaced. Undeterred by the dire threats issued by NUMSA head office, the thirteen, supported by the overwhelming majority of workers, stepped up a campaign in the first instance to protect their right to determine their plant-level leadership but also to stop the changes in their contracts.

It was resolved to challenge the union's unmandated embracing of VW's flexibility regime. And so the idea of a strike started to gain support, but it would be a unique strike. The workers had no direct gripe against VW. The real problem was the union. And so, their action would have to be to strike against NUMSA. NUMSA stepped up its opposition to the workers. The issue for the bureaucrats was not the erosion of workplace rights and worker control, it was about their ability to show management and government that they were worthy partners, that they could control the work force.

The COSATU general secretary Zwelinzima Vavi arrived in Uitenhage on February 1, 2000. The notice for the meeting that he was due to address makes it clear that COSATU had taken a strong position:

COSATU General Secretary, Zwelinzima Vavi will address a NUMSA General Meeting at Babs Madlakane Hall, Kwanobuhle, Uitenhage, this afternoon at 5 P.M. The meeting has been called by NUMSA to address the illegal strike at the Volkswagen plant in Uitenhage. Vavi will urge all NUMSA members to go back to work and distance themselves from agent provocateurs bent on disturbing production from the plant.

At the subsequent CCMA hearing it was revealed that his flight from Johannesburg was paid for by VWSA.

Emboldened by NUMSA and COSATU support, VW management indicated that they were prepared to close down the plant until stability was achieved and that the export order would be transferred to European plants. In Cape Town, President Thabo Mbeki was making some last-minute changes to his state of the nation parliamentary address. He singled out the VWSA strike as being illegal and unjustified and warned that the ANC's "standing in the eyes of the investor community cannot be held hostage by elements pursuing selfish and anti-social purposes." He informed the nation that "the government has worked with management at Volkswagen as well as NUMSA to ensure that the problem created by some irresponsible elements at this plant is resolved. The government will not waver from this position." In the same speech, Mbeki heaped praised upon the thirteen corporate multimillionaires who made up his International Investment Council (IIC). These included Jurgen Schrempp of Daimler Chrysler, Citigroup Vice President William Rhodes, Minoru Makihara of Mitsubishi, and international financier George Soros.

Immediately after Mbeki's speech, armed riot police descended upon Uitenhage. One report at the time described the city in the following way: "Heavily armed soldiers have been stationed on the routes normally used by the strikers. The police routinely follow strikers and committee members, stop them without reason and question them. At 3 A.M. last Thursday, March 2, troops cordoned off a section of Kwanobuhle, home to many of the 6,000-strong work force. Armed police then began a systemic house-to-house search that ended with two arrests—one for cannabis possession and one for failure to appear in court on an unspecified charge."

For weeks the workers met every second day in the community hall. Initially solidarity was strong and VW struggled to get replacement labor from the surrounding community. However unemployment was endemic and community members broke ranks by taking jobs. Soon only a hard core of a hundred strikers or so were still coming to meetings. They would put their faith in the courts.

Those in the union hierarchy who tried to start a debate on the issue were dealt with harshly. Dinga Sikwebu, the union's education officer, was fired for distributing a mildly critical discussion document on the VWSA debacle as a basis for debate within the union. His dismissal was effected a few days before he was to challenge for the position of general secretary.

After being reinstated, he lost a close contest for this position.

The Council for Conciliation, Mediation, and Arbitration (CCMA) ruled that the workers had to be reinstated as their dismissal was procedurally unfair. But the workers' joy was short-lived. Making its way through higher courts, the Labor Appeal Court finally held that, since the strike was illegal, it would be unfair for the company to have to reinstate or compensate them just because there had been some instances of unfairness in the process of dismissing them. Television news reports showed workers emerging from the hearing wearing the T-shirts of a new union they had formed, sobbing, their struggle crushed.

Meanwhile retrenchments, outsourcing, and a general rollback of worker rights continued apace in the motor industry. Matt Gennrich, the general manager of VWSA, explained how the company cashed in on exports by using the government's Motor Industry Development Program (MIDP). At exactly the same time, NUMSA was blaming the cynical use of the MIDP by Nissan South Africa for the retrenchment of 360 workers at its Rosslyn plant in June 2001.

In the *NUMSA News* of June 2001, Alec Erwin, minister of trade and industry and once education officer of NUMSA, explained the government's position and what they expected from the union: "Our target is to persuade international investors to invest here . . . But if you lose a whole factory like VW, it is a major problem. You don't know how much damage that [the strike] did . . . We had to send cabinet ministers to Germany on the VW dispute to convince them. At the beginning of this year, the president met top VW people. Their concern—'your best union can't hold its factories.'" At the same time Erwin heaped scorn on attempts to stop job losses—"to say our strategy is 'we'll stop the job losses,' it's like the king who thought he could stop the sea, and the sea took him. It is not in our power to stop it."

Politicians with power. Union bureaucrats waiting for deployment within government. Janus-faced officials appearing concerned in the presence of ordinary workers while rather enjoying the hard macro-language they can talk in caucuses with bosses. Shop stewards crushed for resisting the yank of their officials to anti-worker economic imperatives. But there's also a story of workers pioneering new ways and forms of struggle, dimly recalling traditions of militancy and guile. Ultimately this was a strike against the ANC's economic policies and the union movement's cynical acquiescence. The workers lost but the message was out.

The Uitenhage strike did allow for a few lessons. Political parties entered the fray, opportunistically. The PAC, the UDM, and the obscure and ever-splitting Trotskyist group, Workers International Vanguard League (WIVL), all traipsed through Uitenhage with plans to capitalize on the struggle. As time went by, workers were cut off from real community support. Many good people in the Uitenhage community and beyond became susceptible to propaganda that there was a "political agenda" behind the strike. With the unemployment rate at over 60 percent, it was important to build bridges with the community, the religious organizations and the like. Isolated and feeling the effects of a long strike (workers had lost their houses, furniture was repossessed and children were going hungry), workers stopped meeting as a collective and came to rely entirely on the legal process.

Almost at the time the Labor Appeal Court was writing its judgment against the VW workers, a strike broke out at the Engen plant in the South Basin of Durban. With demands rooted in the issues confronting the community as a whole, this strike took an entirely different turn.

ENGEN IS THE SOUTH AFRICAN AFFILIATE of the oil multinational, Exxon. Its huge oil refinery sits like a giant, crashed spaceship less than 50 meters from the first row of houses in the Durban township of Wentworth. Wentworth, reserved by apartheid planners for colored South Africans, is home to about 20,000 people. Unemployment is extremely high. Engen is the single biggest employer in what are regarded as the traditional "colored" occupations of boiler making, fitting and turning, mill wrighting, pipe fitting, and similar artisan work.

Indeed, the Engen Training Center (which the company boasts demonstrates its commitment to community upliftment) provides training only in these disciplines. In this way, it ensures a ready supply of labor during the one time of the year when the refinery becomes really labor-intensive, the annual turnaround. At this time thousands of temporary workers are badged up, given a short induction course, and then stream on-site to repair pipes and refurbish valves. Things must move fast; they only have six weeks in which to overhaul many million tons of steel.

In the past, Engen used to hire the turnaround people directly. However, after a slightly more progressive Labor Relations Act came into effect in 1995, it has been reluctant to accept responsibility for the workers it uses. One reason is that workers die on the plant every year. The highly unstable catalyst hydroflouric acid, used in the production process, normally claims victims during the shutdown. While South African law offers unheard of protection to corporations for injuries on duty (only allowing a company to be sued for patrimonial loss, which they can well afford to pay), the legal paperwork is onerous and the death of an Engen worker can look pretty bad in the press.

Second, in order to satisfy foreign investors that its manpower to output ratio is within limits that would attract portfolio managers, it likes to keep its books clean of employees. Last, but most important, using labor brokers to split up its huge workforce into a number of different disconnected units, allows Engen to avoid its obligations in terms of labor law. If any of these sets of workers unionize and tries to bargain for better wages, it can simply cancel the contract it has with that labor broker, effectively dismissing the workers. There are many hungry recruits waiting to take their place. If it was the employer, it could never get away with this type of blatant union bashing.

Notwithstanding these tactics, workers have pulled strikes more or less every year during turnaround and won small victories here and there. In 1997, workers demanded more safety watchers on site, something reluctantly conceded by management only after a crippling and violent seven day strike that cost R300,000 per day in wasted shipping costs alone. The community also paid a price. In order to keep the strike going, scab labor had to be vigorously discouraged. A youngster from the community trying to sneak home after a stint of replacement labor was stabbed and died. Several others were badly beaten.

In May 2001, another strike at Engen was looming that would affect almost everyone in the Wentworth community. As residents of Wentworth themselves admit, in the most self- critical terms, the community is known for its fractiousness. The union that had the task of holding together workers and community was named CEIWU; its members disagree about what exactly the acronym stands for. It's either the Construction, Engineering and Industrial Workers Union or else the words Chemical and Energy also feature somewhere. On Friday, May 18, union members met in their dingy office next to a makeshift township hairdresser in Wentworth.

Jane Smith was dressed in big boots and an overall that seemed to overwhelm her. The big male artisans with Popeye-like forearms around her only served to emphasize her small physique. The meeting was rowdy and tense. Suddenly Jane started to speak. Silence rippled through the room. Some men turned toward her but most just put their heads down and listened. The message was simple and to the point: "For too long our people have been messed around by Engen. Our parents have died waiting for a better deal from Engen. It is time we stood up and gave ourselves a more secure future. It is time to fight.

"This time, there must be no violence against our own people," Jane implored. The strike committee members seemed unconvinced. I heard a pair of knuckles crack somewhere in the room. "What they are doing is wrong, by working while we struggle. But we must focus all our anger against the real enemy, not the weak among us. Or have we also become too scared ourselves to challenge the Goliath that is oppressing us?" There was a perceptible change in the mood of the meeting as she drove home the point with this reference to the Bible.

Jane Smith is 27 years old. She is a single mom with two children. She is passionate about the issues of wage parity, which is one of the central points of this brewing strike. With the introduction of new rates many workers would take home less than the year before. The strikers demand that turnaround workers get paid at the same rate as the permanent workers. But for Jane it is more than a pay dispute. It is about the pollution that she believes has already damaged her children's lungs. It is about security of employment and about building a sense of leadership in the community. And, as I was to discover later, this strike was not the means to win some or other demand. To some extent the strike was an end in itself. It was about striking back.

I TOOK A DRIVE AROUND WENTWORTH with Jane later that Friday night. Most flats are in a profound state of disrepair. The early evening air was thick with sulphur. It chokes the uninitiated and brings tears to the eyes. Groups of people hung around outside the flats. Most get jobs for a month or two at Engen and then get laid off. Jane confirmed what I already knew: that Engen does no employing itself but uses labor brokers and so takes no responsibility for the terms of employment. Many of the labor brokers are themselves from the community and so the anger turns inwards. Jane tells me that, in an attempt to widen decision making, the workers have invited prominent members of the community to be on their negotiating team. A joint body has been formed called the Industrial Relations Forum and although it is new, she has high hopes for its success. Her hopes are realized because the IR Forum, from then on, operated as the equivalent of the resident associations in the other areas.

The next meeting was opposite the Engen plant on Saturday, May 19. Workers poured out into the parking lot. One of the organizers told the crowd that their grievances were long-standing but they should still try to mediate. The meditation is set up for that Saturday. But it collapses because, according to Des D'Sa, the brand new chair of the IR Forum and longtime community activist (himself dismissed from a chemical company in the South Basin for union activity), the management wanted to watch a rugby game.

By Monday's lunchtime meeting, on May 21, anger is high. Engen's new gambit is to refuse to negotiate at all. It is not the employer, it says. If the labor brokers don't supply the workers at the given rates, it will find others, even if labor has to be sourced further afield. It issues pamphlets alleging, "Wentworth will be the Loser!" The workers decide it is time to stop working. There are no dissenting voices. They send delegates into the plant to spread the news. It is an awesome decision for many of the workers as these two months of employment are all they will have for the year. But they say they are *gatvol* (fed up). Although they obviously need the money, there seems to be some unnamed thing that makes working for Engen this year intolerable. According to sworn statements made by the company later on, those workers who walked off shift in response to the strike call, "systematically" smashed windows, damaged vehicles, and committed casual industrial sabotage. I was at Engen on that day, and was besieged by working folk showing me their pay slips and their pathetic take-home pay after tax deductions.

The following day, May 22, there was another meeting, this time on the sportsfield behind Engen. By this time every single turnaround worker was in attendance. As a show of solidarity, workers began handing in the badges necessary to gain access to the Engen site, placing them in a big brown sack. I could not get over the huge amount of people present. The pitch was overflowing with well over 2,000 workers, many of them with their wives. Some brought their teenage sons, keen for action. There was only a loud hailer for public address but the crowd was quiet and pressed close together. It was decided that the strike would continue until Engen capitulated, no less, and that people should go home for the day but return early the next morning to begin a roving picket in Tara Road outside the refinery.

Events started to spiral quickly from there. As she left the sportsground, Jane Smith, with other union leaders and officials, were swooped upon by a squad of police cars. They were arrested on ridiculous charges. The local police, long accused of being in Engen's pocket, had secretly filmed the mass meeting and then provided Engen with footage of the badges being handed in and the chant of "Fuck Engen" that had gone up. This was evidence, they contended, of an intent to enter the premises and commit industrial sabotage. Simultaneously, Engen launched a number of High Court interdicts against the union and its leaders, also seeking costs against these people. Even I was caught up in events and found my name in court papers as one of the alleged troublemakers.

With all its resources, this multinational corporation seemed to want to crush the strike by getting workers to fight all sorts of other defensive battles. But workers committed whatever cash they had for bail money and Jane and the other leaders were released on bail later on that Tuesday night. The events of the day were widely reported on local radio stations, in the local daily press, and on national TV. Amazingly, the coverage was sympathetic. Somebody in Wentworth apparently took the time to explain the background to the strike to the journalists very patiently.

ON WEDNESDAY EVENING, May 23, 2001, the Austerville community hall is full. Jane Smith is demure and unruffled by the day in the holding cell of the notorious Wentworth police station. By now the issues have become bigger and a broad range of community leaders are present. Ex- MK fighter Derek McBride is in one corner lending his support. A community welfare organization leader complains about the arrests. "They refuse to arrest their drug lord friends and all the rapists, but arrest our union leaders. We've had enough of their corruption." A placard on the stage reads, "Engen / Police Collusion heading for Collision." Professor Fatima Meer of the CCG has been invited to speak and she rails against Engen's arrogance. She also gently scolds the COSATU regional chairperson who has been invited to attend the meeting. "Why is COSATU so quiet these days?" Maybe because he sees such immense recruitment potential in the hall, the COSATU bigwig gives a militant speech, threatening sympathy strikes. How amazing, that CEIWU, an insignificant and tiny independent union, can pull a strike like this but COSATU affiliates cannot.

A speaker from the nearby white suburb on the Bluff, has also arrived to give support. She receives rapturous applause for her short and unambiguous message. "Community of Wentworth, what they are doing to you is wrong, we support your fight against Engen."

Reggie, one of the workers, takes to the stage. In a speech, replete with Durban slang, he talks of laboring at Engen for over two decades. He talks of exploitation, of being pushed around, and the hurt of still having to find employment again and again every year through a labor broker, being "inducted" anew each time into a plant he built. It is a moving speech that he translates himself into Zulu for the benefit of the African "chargehands" of a particular labor broker who have just joined the strike after walking off the night shift. They form a bright blue knot in the back of the hall where they stand in their overalls. Spirits are unbelievably high. I feel transported back into the 1980s and the meetings of righteous anger against apartheid that abounded. A member of the Cape Town gang of metalworkers brought down to assist on the shut, pledges his crew's support for the strike. He speaks in Afrikaans and the message is translated into English and Zulu. They will lose pay but count on the solidarity of their Wentworth brothers and (with a charmingly rueful glance at Jane behind him on the stage) . . . er . . . sisters when they confront their employers in Saldanha Bay in the new year.

But the highlight of the meeting is when a priest of the local Roman Catholic church says that the rejection of mediation by the company forces on the agenda the need for passive resistance. In his prayer, he says, "O Lord, we know that if your beloved son, Jesus Christ, was alive in human form in our sinful world today, he would be amongst us, O Lord. He was not a rich man. Jesus was a carpenter, Lord, and he was an artisan. And when he came upon hypocrisy and cheating in your holy house, he used those rough hands to turn the tables and throw the evil- doers out. Lord, give us the strength to act with courage and obedience to your will in these difficult times as we strive to protect the integrity of our homes and our community. We ask this in the name of Jesus Christ, Our Savior, Amen."

After the speeches, workers want to know if reports that Jane and others had been arrested are true. People want to know where their badges are. The police confiscated them. Outpourings of anger are expressed against the police. Suddenly somebody jumps up and says, "Let's go get our badges." It is about ten o'clock at night but such is the feeling among all that the suggestion makes perfect sense. Almost as a single body, the entire meeting marches to the police station two hundred meters away. It is an oddly silent march. As they approach the police station a barrage of stones, bricks, sticks and other objects is let fly. This assault goes on for about twenty minutes before the first reinforcements arrive. Not a single window in the Wentworth police station is unbroken. Several police vans are overturned and smashed. Holed up in the second floor of the station, policemen take pot shots into the night with live ammunition and tear gas.

Miraculously, no one is seriously hurt. Fatima Meer is bundled into a car narrowly escaping injury as the police fusillade thuds into the ground near where she stood. As the wailing sirens of reinforcement are heard, young and old, men and women, workers and family members melt into the night and with the dust of stones still on their hands, make their way home. It is the strangest and yet, in a sense, most natural ending to any meeting I have attended in the new South Africa.

THE NEXT DAY, May 24, 2001, Engen held a press conference at the Durban Country Club, probably the city's most elite venue, the retreat of Natal's erstwhile colonial overlords. It was a different world from the Austerville community hall. According to Engen a few agitators had created the trouble. They could not accept mediation because they were "downsizing." They excitedly lamented the damage done to the police station as if to say, "See the kind of people who we have to deal with?" But their spokesperson was also clearly unsure why exactly he was having to answer one hostile question after another from the press. At tea, a television journalist asks the general manager, a brash Texan, why he didn't want trade unions on site. Both off- guard and arrogant, John Mackay blurts out: "That refinery is owned by an American corporation. I will not, repeat not, allow some ridiculous South African laws to override my obligation to make money for Exxon and its shareholders."

While Engen could not count on the total support of the press, it could do so in respect of the state. The army moved into Wentworth. Using apartheid-era security legislation, they justified this action by saying that the oil refinery was a "National Key-Point." The army threatened to shoot anyone who approached the plant without legitimate business. Youngsters who I spoke to scoffed at this. "It's just show, anyone who wants to burn Engen down can do it quite easily without coming close."

On the same day as the conference, the police arrested a number of people, seemingly at random, for the attack on the police station. One man, Peter Usher, was severely assaulted by the police during the arrest. Suffering broken bones in the arrest, he was encouraged by the police to start running away from the blows that were raining down so that they could shoot him. It was important not to appear chastened by these events and so the core IR Forum activists, now numbering over a hundred, started planning for a rally the next day, that afternoon, with the police out knocking on doors, looking for some of them.

Engen too was active, reminding those whom they patronized what their largesse had provided: school sports team kits, a training center, handouts to a women's abuse center, and a couple of bursaries for kids from the area. They took out huge adverts in the newspaper and bought slots on East Coast Radio alternatively threatening and cajoling. But the effects of the strike were being keenly felt. Through the backdoor they provided the resources to the labor brokers to satisfy most of the demands originally made by the strikers. In particular, they made a written offer to underwrite wage parity.

Their PR efforts did not work inside Wentworth. The distance between the corporation and the community was enormous. One got the sense that somehow the community had found a collective voice, leaders had emerged, and there was a greater sense of purpose. Compromises were not necessary at this stage as a once anonymous community who had previously only appeared in the news in crime stories, were reveling in the strike as a means to voice all their frustrations and hopes. When I pointed out to one of the community leaders that they had won the strike and could just as well call it off, his answer confounded me: "We are not striking for demands, we are striking for dignity." I told him that Engen could not provide "dignity." "Exactly, my friend, exactly!" was his answer.

The next night a candle-light vigil was held outside the refinery. Where did people get the energy to organize and attend so many meetings? This time, middle-class folk who perhaps once lived in the area or have family there also came to the protest. The Anglican archbishop of Natal, the Right Reverend Rubin Phillip, was also there at the head of the procession, as was at least one UniCity Councillor, the CCG's Preggie Naidoo of Isipingo. They linked arms with Des D'Sa, now a wanted man and literally on the run from the police for his prominent role in the rolling mass action. Solemnly, the throng of about 2,000 people snaked down Alabama and into Tara Road, holding their living lights against the cold, neon glare of the massive, many-tiered corporation in the distance. I have witnessed many marches. Few have been more disarming of the enemy than when the soaring voices of children and old ladies set off against the slightly embarrassed baritones of the workers began to sing the Lord's Prayer, the crowd now in a huddle at Engen's main entrance. Every man but one in the two lines of private security that stood behind Engen's giant gates averted their eyes as the words of the prayer reached them:

Forgive us our trespasses, just as we forgive those who trespass
against us.
Lead us not into temptation,
And deliver us from Engen. Amen.

The strike lasted another full week as Engen found itself dragged to the
mediation table by inches. What was initially a strategic gambit had now
become a principled demand: to get Engen itself to the table. As soon as
Engen agreed to this, negotiations were conducted until the early hours of
the morning at the nearby Clairwood racecourse. The session was fraught
with hostility, and labor mediator Chris Brunton only dared to bring the
parties into the same room for a few minutes and then thought better of it.
At the end, Engen agreed to pay all the striking workers for the time the
strike endures. Certain of those it absolutely did not want back on-site, the
alleged "troublemakers," were to be paid off as if they had worked the
entire shutdown. A separate process to address wage parity, backdated to
the date of the shutdown, was also composed.

Just as the agreement was to be signed at around about 1:30 A.M. on June
1, 2001 and to the exasperation of even the lawyer the IR Forum had brought
in to advise on legal technicalities, the workers presented one final demand.
This whole deal hinged now on one last issue. Engen must agree to take back
into its employ Peter Usher, the man assaulted by the police. The rest of the
people on the troublemaker list could remain, but Peter Usher must come
off. It was a demand that seemed to mock not only Engen but the whole conciliation process. Nevertheless, an Engen delegation, unbelieving that everything could falter over just one man, gave in and Peter Usher, a symbol both
of the vicious unfairness of the broader system and the arbitrariness of
Engen's list, was taken off the list of official troublemakers.

The end of the strike was not exactly greeted with jubilation by workers
but there was satisfaction. Together with a mysterious pipeline burst nearby Wentworth, the strike had caused a national shortage of diesel up-coun-
try. Irate motorists waited in long queues in Gauteng at the pumps. A
month later, on radio, the director general of mineral and energy affairs
assured the public that alternative measures were being put in place and
lamented that it was difficult to avoid the shortage: "People have the right
to strike, don't they?"

The strike at Engen, unlike that at VWSA, did not take seriously the conciliation and other legal measures afforded in post-apartheid South Africa.

It relied on timing a wildcat strike to fit in with the company turnaround when the company was most vulnerable. A considerable amount of energy was devoted to building community support while at the same time ensuring that the mobilizations neither became a captive of one political tendency or cast itself in dogmatic ideological terms. As a journalist colleague of mine remarked, "It was as if the whole of Wentworth was on strike." The casualization of labor, that meant workers only received wages for two months of the year, the labor brokering system that meant that they were not regarded as Engen workers and therefore were not eligible for any benefits—these issues were all linked to the fact that the families could not meet escalating rent, water, and electricity costs and were thus being evicted or cut off. Unlike other places around Durban, a corporation was the evildoer in the first instance and not the local state. This did not stop the community from confronting the state when it took sides against them.

The executive of CEIWU did not simply dictate the pace and nature of the struggle but devolved their organization into a loose and very broad grouping of activists and community and religious leaders. The unemployed (some would say "gangsters") were represented at the discussions and their inclusion played a crucial role in cutting off Engen's ability to recruit scabs. All the time the workers tried to ensure that Engen was totally isolated from reaching potential allies in the community, by the IR Forum "getting there first" in the information battle and creating space for various interest groups to become part of the strike committee. For much of the time the union and community structures appeared as one. Nothing demonstrates this better than the fact that the company went after a non-worker, Des D'Sa, in its attempts to interdict the strike rather than, say, Jane Smith or other worker leaders.

The union/community axis avoided the long bureaucratic initial conciliation measures demanded by labor law that have the tendency to siphon off militance and resources. Such energies went to build a strong and involved power base that used car cavalcades, calls for national boycotts of Engen, the construction of a myriad of alliances, lots of meetings and a barrage of press statements instead. The union and community were always keen to send a delegate to happenings in Chatsworth or Mpumulanga. In this regard, Derek McBride played a very important role. However, after the strike, the component parts of the IR Forum were reabsorbed to some extent into their traditional organizations, with the union itself taking on more of the day-to-day work of a trade union. It is only with the coming to town of the World Conference Against Racism that the IR Forum, though not under this name, came back to life again.

I left Wentworth on the morning of July 2, 2001, as throngs of blue-overalled workers, each carrying his own plastic toolbox, clocked in at the main gate, with the strong impression that the strike had not been, first and foremost, about winning the demands I had heard uttered during that very first meeting in the drab CEIWU office with Jane and a coterie of shop stewards two weeks before. It was a method through which many people living in Wentworth acquired a kind of self-consciousness and used this as a basis to fight, during that fortnight, for the way they thought the world ought to be.

1   Peter Rachleff, "The Current Crisis of the South African Labor Movement," www.labournet.de, January 2001.

16. chatsworth reignites

AT ABOUT THE TIME that the strike at Engen began, Chatsworth residents
heard that the Durban High Court had effectively ordered that Thulisile
Manqele's water be disconnected again. The battleground was moving from
the courts and back to Chatsworth. But now more innovative and direct
forms of action began to unfold. Responding to electricity and water cutoffs,
residents of the council flats met to plan. After a heated meeting, they
moved en masse to the home of a local DA councilor and disconnected his
electricity and water, a tactic that was later also dramatically used by Soweto residents against their mayor. A journalist from the city's evening newspaper, Krisendra Bisetty, summed up sentiments at the meeting:

> More than 300 tenants of council-owned flats in Westcliff and
> Bayview vowed at a meeting yesterday to resist moves by the council
> to disconnect water and electricity supplies because of unpaid bills
> and to occupy the homes of local councilors.
>
> Significantly, they have the support of residents in three other
> Durban suburbs—Wentworth, Isipingo and Mpumalanga where sim-
> ilar problems are being experienced.
>
> Unicity Mayor Obed Mlaba, who was not aware of the looming
> trouble, last night expressed surprise that the situation "has
> reached that level where people are going to take the law into the
> own hands." Mlaba warned residents to expect the law to take its
> course if things got out of hand.
>
> In a day of high drama, the tenants were bussed after the meet-
> ing to the Chatsworth home of local Democratic Alliance councilor
> Mr. Rocky Naidoo, who was, however, not there. It was just as well,
> because some angry tenants, who stormed the building and banged
> on the windows, threatened to lynch him. They took out their frus-
> tration on a neighbor, hurling abuse on the startled man who had
> apparently criticized them.

The tenants earlier resolved to:

- Occupy the homes of Naidoo and Minority Front councilor Mr. Visvin Reddy who is an executive member of the Unicity Council. They vowed to remain there until their grievance is resolved.

- Occupy the office of the council's director of housing, Mr. Sbu Gumede, who has allegedly not found time to listen to their grievance; and

- Form a band of mobile "defenders of communities" who would race to houses where the electricity supply was being disconnected. They plan to confront and "chase away" the city technicians.

The organizers, who launched their intensified campaign in a church hall, want their action to be in the form of passive, militant resistance. Residents have already been flouting the law and illegally reconnecting electricity supplies.

Orlean Naidoo said the tenants' struggle was going on for three years. "When you live in poor communities, there is a lot of disregard shown at you. Some residents who were employed as cleaners by the council paid R14 a day on bus fares and earned R22 a day. They can't afford to put food on the table."

Mr. Derick McBride, representing the Wentworth community, said: "We believe that to deprive us of the right to water is an act of violence." In Mpumalanga, people were being deprived of basic rights, local community leader Mr. Sbu Zamisa said, adding that to fight "unjust moves" by the council was to be met with a police and military force. "That says to us that the council has already declared war on poor people. They are treating us as they don't know the socioeconomic conditions which we are living under," Zamisa said.

Mlaba said that to get 6,000 liters of free water a month, consumers had to sign an acknowledgment of debt for a special cutoff mechanism to be installed. "If people do not acknowledge that procedure and policies, we have no choice in some cases but to take drastic action."

Mlaba, however, questioned the role of pressure groups, saying that apart from highlighting issues, they did not solve problems.

Rocky Naidoo, meanwhile, said he would only meet with people "with an open agenda. You don't just rock up at a person's house with a mob." Naidoo said the power box at his house was tampered with. (*Daily News,* May 21, 2001)

This kind of direct action became part of the strategies of the civic struggles across the country. The SECC, in an impressive march and occupation, arrived at the home of Johannesburg mayor Amos Masondo and dug up his electricity cables.

At the same time the CCG went on the offensive in response to the government's claim of free water. A few days after the "direct action" in Chatsworth the CCF put out a press statement that called the 6 free kiloliter policy "a pack of lies." The pamphlet went on to say:

Yes, there is a six free kiloliter policy in the UniCities. But only those with means will benefit. This is because people with any arrears (by definition, the poors) will not get a drop for free. Until they pay up. In many cases this includes water, electricity and rent arrears and so, for the truly poor, the first six kiloliters comes at the immodest price of, what, R15,000.00.

The pamphlet continued:

We must also deflate the "come to the UniCity offices and make arrangements to pay" fib. In Durban this means to be required to sign an acknowledgment of debt which allows the attachment of property without much further legal process after three, six, twelve months if those arrears are still not paid. Then, if you own your house you are evicted on- the-quick and new residents installed. The six free kiloliters is, for the nearly indigent, an administrative and credit-control plot.

After the events in Mpumalanga and with telephone calls requesting CCG chapters to be formed in Kwa-Dukuza, Umlazi, Shongweni and Umkomaas, it was decided to draw all these diverse struggles into one organization. The Concerned Citizens Forum (CCF) was launched with the participation of 24 organizations at the Workers' College in July 2001. Tragically, in the midst of these developments, Preggie Naidoo died of a massive heart attack. The CCF was immediately thrown into an election battle for the vacant Isipingo seat. The stakes were high as the main political organizations—the DA, the

IFP, and the ANC pumped huge resources into the area to win the seat. The young upstart, the CCF, had to be crushed. The CCF supported independent candidate, IDF member and choice of those living in the flats of Lotus and Orient Park, Angie Pakkiri. There were eleven candidates in all.

The CCF had learned from the election campaign a few months before. Angie stood on a non-racial platform with a defiant message against evictions, and water and electricity disconnections. In one open-air speech she explained why she believed the ANC, the DA and the IFP were all really one party. They had the same "right wing economic policy" that could only succeed at the expense of the poor. She won by a 30 percent margin.

17. global and local: the world conference against racism and the durban social forum

THE CONCERNED CITIZENS' FORUM, from its modest beginnings in Fatima Meer's initiative to draw Chatsworth voters toward the ANC, soon grew to include more than 20 new community movements from all over kwaZulu-Natal. The inner life of these militant community movements could be described, if they were a single person, as being manic-depressive. Brief spurts of intense activity ahead of, say, an eviction, give way, when the danger is over, to weeks in which more mundane concerns of life and love take over. Besides bonds of friendship and dealing with the debts incurred each time buses are hired, there was little that connected those working in the Durban city center with people in Mpumalanga or Chatsworth during times of downturn.

The same goes for contact between people in the townships themselves. Even when people intended to meet more often, other events frequently interrupted the cycles of struggle and organization building, like religious holidays or a patch of witheringly hot weather. Activism remained essentially reactive. Perhaps this is the new way. No domineering, bureaucratic organization whose constitution demanded all sorts of rituals and loyalties existed. When there was no need for the shield that the CCF provided, it was laid to one side and the people that made it up assumed other roles. To be part of an organization did not demand the wearing of lapel badges or the carrying of party cards. One didn't need to be glum and driven and Jehovah Witness–like, ever trying to win recruits among those sinfully enjoying themselves in shebeens, on the soccer fields, playing cards, or making out in the alleys where the lights are dim. But when the state made a move, the organizational activity in response was frenzied and imbued with that clarity of purpose, invention, and self-sacrifice that distinguishes the best of us in emergencies.

It was in one of these periods of relative lull, in June 2001, that the media began to highlight a forthcoming United Nations conference—to give it its full name, the UN World Conference on Racism, Racial Discrimination, Xenophobia, and other related forms of intolerance (WCAR). The venue for this gathering was to be Durban's ultra-posh International Convention Centre.

The inter-governmental conference would run from September 1 to 6. Just before that, beginning in the last week of August, there would be a similarly large congregation of international non-governmental organizations (NGOs) working in the fields of race and identity. This NGO Forum put together by personnel from South Africa's national civil society coordinating body, the South African NGO Coalition (SANGOCO), had been handed large sums of money by the European Union to get this parallel show on the road.

This was in fact the third World Conference Against Racism held by the UN. The first two were held in Geneva in 1978 and 1983. Both had been brought about by pressures from Third World governments, both condemned apartheid in South Africa, both were boycotted by the United States. The third WCAR was initiated in a different political context. Apartheid had been consigned to history. After the end of the Cold War, the West was no longer as willing to address the concerns of the Third World. The fight against racial inequality had been taken up by the anti-globalization movement that had exploded into prominence with the protests against the World Trade Organization meeting in Seattle in 1999, while many Third World governments had become discredited as champions of the oppressed. Unlike in 1978 and 1983, much of the momentum for the conference came from NGOs, meeting at the parallel forum as supposed "representatives of civil society." The preparations for the conference included a determined effort to place the demand for reparations for slavery and colonialism on the global agenda.

South Africa had been approached to host the WCAR—in the words of the government announcement—"in view of South Africa's experience in defeating institutionalized racism and the processes put in place for a peaceful transformation to democracy and reconciliation." For Western governments the South African "miracle" was the ideal way of conveying that racism was on the retreat. The South African government was willing to take its share of the credit. It would, doubtless, try to use both these forums as an opportunity to boost its image as the paragon of non-racialism and egalitarianism.

Many in the CCF, exposed to the ANC's economic policies that, but for a small crony elite, actually entrenched white control of the wealth and deepened Black misery, started talking about holding protest action to make these very points. It might also be a good idea, some said, to use these conferences as an opportunity to bind together all the different cords that made up the CCF, to mobilize for once as a united organization, to be proactive.

THROUGH JULY AND AUGUST 2001, a range of meetings were held at the Workers' College in Bolton Hall, one of Durban's famous trade union meeting venues from the past. The growth of the CCF and its success in staving off evictions placed it at the center of these discussions. It was here where an entirely new strategy would be determined. Necessarily, discussions occurred mainly between delegates from the communities who attended these meetings and these could no longer occur as broadly and directly as before, at the barricades, so to speak. Nevertheless delegations remained quite large with an area like Chatsworth sending about twenty people to Workers' College meetings. Sometimes sharp disputes arose around which strategies were best. The only voting that was ever necessary was whether decisions would be taken by voting or by consensus. The latter option won the day. But differences remained. At one stage a CCF stalwart suggested that the organization simply ask to have a delegate address the conference for a few minutes, recording their concerns. Mass action should only be considered if this was not allowed. Finally a plan emerged that gained everyone's consent. There were to be two distinct phases to the way the CCF dealt with the conference.

In the weeks preceding the inter-governmental conference, there would be gatherings in each of the CCF townships. Here local issues would be related to—or interpreted in line with—the theme of the conference. The interpretive work needed to be done. The WCAR was not a bread-and-butter issue. This was a time when a political course was being urged, mainly by the City-based members of the CCF, that was not as urgent and self-evident to everyone living, say, in Chatsworth as resisting an eviction.

Also, an ideological offensive assumed a common ideology among those who made up the CCF, and this was an issue that had, deliberately, never been clarified. After the cannon-fodder approach to politics that many people had suffered at the hands of either Inkatha or the so-called liberation movements, it was no wonder that these ideas were treated with some suspicion at first. Why go to Durban and march for or against a conference? Those are politicians' issues.

After much discussion at the Workers' College, it was agreed that engaging with other communities and, for that matter, with the powers-that-be on the terrain of the WCAR was a necessary step to take. Whether this opinion, in turn, was debated thoroughly within the community movements is hard to say. But once the delegations to the Workers' College meetings, comprising people like Derek McBride, Angie Pakkiri, Sipho Mlaba, Brandon Pillay, Maxwell Cele, and Orlean Naidoo, gave the nod, community participation in future events was enthusiastic.

From the beginning, it was clear that the WCAR mobilizations would, to a certain extent, be opportunistic. While most CCF members were, in their bones, anti-racists too, it would be fair to say that the dominant motive in pulling together public demonstrations during the race conference was to exploit the platform this provided to make telling points about class. CCF activists realized they would have to do a lot of work to explain to foreigners that, despite the superficial, if dramatic, advances that had been made on the race front in South Africa, these did not compensate for the deepening misery of the majority of the poor (and Black) people of this country. Even if they failed to make a dent in the epistemological wall that hides evidence of South Africa's failed revolution, actions during the WCAR would be an ideal test of strength against a government that was bound to recommence evictions and cutoffs as the last delegates boarded their Boeings home.

The second phase of the CCF plan was to organize a massive and unequivocally militant demonstration to be held the day the conference officially opened. While giving support to radical international causes, this march would attack the ANC for its Thatcherite policies and expose its hypocrisy on the question of race. An even more important decision was taken. In early August 2001, Mandla Sishi, secretary of the CCF, was given the unanimous nod to reach out to other organizations elsewhere in the country and to broaden the planned protest action. A national act was to be committed.

PEOPLE FROM OUT OF TOWN, free-floating left-wingers, those involved in Palestinian solidarity work, and those involved in community movements in Gauteng and Cape Town, were contacted. Encouragingly, they too were committed to stage protest actions. Was there a basis for a joint effort? After further discussion, the name of the organization sponsoring the joint protests was chosen: the Durban Social Forum, or DSF. The name gestured respectfully and militantly towards the Genoa Social Forum which, only months before, had presided over the biggest anti-capitalist demonstrations Europe had seen, perhaps, since 1968. Durban community activists wanted to be part of this broad movement.

The DSF was no political party although it did tend to privilege membership of actually existing mass-based community movements and strongly discouraged sectarianism. Yet lines had to be drawn somewhere. Although it was left open whether COSATU or various church formations should be a part of the DSF if they wished, the ANC and SACP were regarded, beneath all the rhetoric, as the mainstays of government policy. As such they were not welcome.

Technology played a crucial role in putting the DSF together, creating connections between people from different regions who had not worked together before. It also acted as a tool of inclusion allowing persons who did not blossom in mass-meeting situations to make their points and contributions. The flurry of e-mails facilitated the contestation of ideas among a large enough group, relaying ideas floating around in various community movements in an open way for any one to read, mull over, and communicate onwards. People were energized and responsive to a new and exciting community in the weeks before the conference.

And so the DSF drew in people from the Cape Town–based Anti-Eviction Campaign, University of Durban-Westville students and faculty, the Soweto Electricity Crisis Committee, Keep Left (a gathering of city-based Johannesburg socialists), and the Anti-Privatization Forum, an umbrella body in Johannesburg that had grown out of parallel struggles against the restructuring of Wits University and the privatization of municipal services in Johannesburg. Also, people now working in what they would term "progressive NGOs" like Jubilee South, the Alternative Information and Development Centre (AIDC) and the National Land Committee (NLC) joined the DSF bringing to it precious resources and, in the case of the last named, an entirely new constituency.

Since the daring invasion of land by hundreds of desperate families at Bredell east of Johannesburg during the winter of 2001, the issue of landlessness had come to occupy some political attention. With South African businesspeople already nervous, often on racist grounds, about land invasions in Zimbabwe, prices on the Johannesburg Stock Exchange fell with the news of the Bredell land invasions, and a national crisis was suddenly in the offing. The land invaded at Bredell was unused. However the question posed by the invasion was whether the ANC would allow redistribution of land outside the very narrow willing-buyer, willing-seller policy parameters that applied to all but a few thousand people with "valid" land claims.

Although the PAC and certain church leaders initially supported the so-called invaders, they were yanked into line by the ruling party with dire threats of arrest. Gauteng-based comrades like Andile Mngxitama from the NLC and Ahmed Variawa and Daniel Hutchinson from Wits University provided principled and practical support with limited resources. Isolated, cold, and under a court injunction to move, this brave intervention upon which many landless South Africans had pinned their tactical hopes, looked set to be crushed. After a visit by the minister of land affairs and the minister of safety and security in their swank Mercedes Benzes, the police swept in efficiently suppressing the invasion and breaking down the shacks.

The National Land Committee had earlier assisted in forming an organization called the Landless People's Movement (LPM), which brought many of the evicted land tenants, "squatters," or otherwise displaced persons on their depressing data-base together as a social force. It was not a tight organization and its members were from disparate rural or peri-urban areas. The LPM might have started life as no more than a discursive necessity in the NLC's fighting for progressive land redistribution policies. Government and commercial farmers could be told, "Look there is a pressure group, a constituency out there that are demanding progress with land reform and the provision of housing." After Bredell, however, this organization swelled in numbers into the thousands and acquired a very visible urban core. With an eye on the WCAR, they launched a campaign declaring simply "Landlessness = Racism." About three thousand of the landless came to Durban by train during the WCAR. After meetings between those involved in the planning of this event and those planning other similar protests, it was decided that the LPM would join the DSF. The demand for land resonated widely, and was taken up in Mpumalanga after Mpumalanga DSF delegates were exposed to the ideas and methods of the LPM.

THE FIRST REAL, united DSF action was not a resounding success, though it might well have seemed to be so. The Palestinian Support Group was an affiliate of the DSF, which included anti-capitalist militants like Palestinian Solidarity Front leader Naeem Jeenah and the erudite and brave former trade union leader and now academic, Salim Vally, as well as some global conspiracy theorists and a large number of Muslim chauvinists. In the spirit of bringing the DSF together as a living, acting entity and participating in good, old-fashioned solidarity work, it was decided to hold a joint rally at the Durban city hall on August 19, 2001. At this rally, people from CCF strongholds would be bused in to join many members of the Muslim faith who had an interest in protesting the oppression of Palestinians but would otherwise not really have much in common with the DSF. The meeting would be run so that local issues as well as events surrounding the Israeli occupation of Palestine could be discussed. Since the Palestinian Support Group would be paying for the buses, it would be an inexpensive way for the CCF to begin meeting as a unit ahead of the WCAR.

In her speech, Fatima Meer attempted to draw linkages between the different struggles and also spoke to the growing South African resistance on its own terms. But the platform was dominated by repetitive, and sometimes embarrassingly fundamentalist, assertions about the second intifadah. No translation into isiZulu was provided and political developments in Mpumalanga, Wentworth, and Chatsworth were given little attention. The result was an excellent meeting in terms of international solidarity with the Palestinian people but a poor meeting in terms of galvanizing local communities ahead of the WCAR. This alienated a few of the commuters and raised suspicions again about whether the constituencies in Chatsworth and Mpumalanga were somehow being "used." But people had already traveled a long enough distance with each other to be able to talk about these problems, and agree that while still building the DSF, it would be better to err on the side of the local rather than the global.

In Wentworth, the remnant of the Industrial Relations Forum that had played such an important role during the Engen strike convened its phase-one meeting. They invited Professor Dennis Brutus, renowned anti-apartheid activist, poet and global anti-debt campaigner, to speak. Tracey Fared, a journalist, does a better job than I could in describing the meeting that took place in the Austerville Community Hall; the same venue that had, a few months earlier, been jammed full of anti-Engen militants. Her article appeared in the official DSF newsletter, produced by the Indy Media Centre South Africa during the WCAR.

> Looking around the hall at the faces of the women and men who had braved the rain to hear Brutus speak, it occurred to me how surprised foreign visitors might be that the very same posters used during the strike were once again lopsidedly prestricked against the walls. "Phansi Engen, Phansi SAPS," "New Apartheid: Rich and Poor,"

"No to Water Cutoffs and Evictions." Who would have thought that forced removals, police violence, and strike-breaking would be, like the poor, still very much among us seven years after 'liberation'? . . . I wondered, how would I explain, say, to a Black friend or comrade from overseas my traitorous actions in joining in the melody and dance of those who, all around me, chastised Mbeki, Mandela, and the once heroic ANC?

"It is pure hypocrisy," Prof. Brutus, explains, his voice carrying the slight twang of decades in exile, "for this government to parade around as if it is the champion of the anti-racist struggle. It is hypocrisy because its very own economic policies continue to hurt Black people, in the most callous fashion." Beckoning for the deafening applause to die down, Brutus continues, "And what's more, the stance of the people with whom I broke stones on Robben Island or waved placards in exile, on international forums is just as disgraceful. They make common cause with naked imperialism and oppose policies that could free the South from global apartheid."

Aware that his last point had only attracted a smattering of applause, Brutus stepped forward from around the podium and slowly approached the audience. Observing the spring in his step, it was hard to imagine that this man, who had once been shot escaping from the security police in the 1960s, was already 77 years old. "I don't think I have explained what I mean, properly," he says, eyes twinkling. "Do you know what this monster is that I like to call "global apartheid"?

"No-oo!" is the answer from the crowd.

"Well," Brutus says, looking ruefully at the chairperson of the meeting, "Do I have some time . . . ?"

By the time we left the meeting, there was a buzz amongst us all like I have never felt before. People were talking to each other. Suddenly so many things made sense. Why our water was getting cut off and our people thrown onto the street. Why our children had to pay school fees or else. Why the local clinic had been closed down. Why Engen had retrenched workers to increase its share price. Why foreign companies are happy to give Yengeni's [4 x 4 cars] to local elites. Why our president doesn't support the intifadah. Why the youth of the North are also out on the streets and why our Minister of Finance hates them so . . .

One did not have to jet all over the world like Dennis to fight global apartheid effectively. One simply has to start building organizations, building power in the communities where one lives—confronting, militantly, the most terrible aspects of your oppression. And after that—one must link up with others around you, all over the world.

The members of the Westcliff Flat Residents Association in Chatsworth had entirely different ideas about their local event. On August 25, 2001, they hosted members of the Soweto Electricity Crisis Committee and representatives of the Dalit People's Movement from India, in town to lobby against the caste system in India during the WCAR. I witnessed the most poignant of meetings where women, indistinguishable from each other in dress and demeanor, some from the slums of Chatsworth and others from Calcutta, exchanged politenesses via a pedantic Hindi translator.

It so happened that, on that very day, a family had been evicted in Block 175, Westcliff. There was no need for a translator as the entire reception party roused themselves and marched in loose formation to the house about 500 meters away, on the way stopping to point out items of interest to the visitors—a river, a temple, a view across the hill into Umlazi. The security guard posted to prevent reentry was chased away, although he seemed to briefly entertain heroic thoughts, having drawn his pistol. But, as we have already seen, guns are not necessarily a match for the women of Chatsworth. The tirade of derision the sentry received, weapon in hand, stung like bullets and he left the scene. What an experience for the foreigners who vigorously wrung the hands of their hosts from Chatsworth as, a few hours later, they said their untranslatable goodbyes.

Camera people from the IMC captured the footage. This could be shown, deftly edited by independent film-maker, Ben Cashdan, later that same evening to those among the slowly assembling DSF contingent who had missed the action. Local newspapers also reported the story. The DSF's campaign of exposing the mercilessness of government policy towards the poor had got off to an unexpectedly good start.

The local Mpumalanga event could not take place in Mpumalanga mainly because of its distance from Durban. So it was brought to Durban's Natal Technikon in the form of a cultural evening combined with one or two fiery orations. Publicized at the NGO Forum, it attracted quite a few curious visitors such as a U.S.-based group called Black Workers for Justice. So impressed were they by proceedings that they made plans the next day to visit Mpumalanga themselves at the invitation of Sipho Mlaba and the CCF. Taxi loads of people from Chatsworth, Isipingo, and Wentworth also pitched up and the show was ready to start. A troupe of *iscathimeya* singers and dancers from Mpumalanga had the small crowd in standing ovation. In between their performances, Sipho Mlaba and Maxwell Cele spoke about conditions in the township and Ben Cashdan showed clips on a big screen from a work in progress.

Once DSF people from other centers arrived in Durban, it was time to start debating exactly what form the march should take. At CCF meetings at the Workers' College, it had been agreed that it would not be acceptable to deal ambiguously with the ANC's role in the neoliberal onslaught against the poor. It was up to CCF participants like Mandla Sishi, Joe Guy, Saranel Benjamin, Mandla Gwala, Heinrich Bohmke, Brandon Pillay, and Ramesh Harcharan to put together as militant a march as consensually possible. This had to be accomplished within the larger ambit of the DSF and was not a major problem since the CCF was on the same wavelength as the SECC and the Anti-Eviction Campaign.

The DSF functioned loosely, as a coordinating body rather than a command center. Its constituent parts like the CCF, SECC, Keep Left, or the Landless People's Movement retained their own identities and, for the most part, adopted positions on various questions in terms of their usual, discrete decision-making processes. The DSF was more like a kitchen than a boardroom, with the people entering this space each contributing an ingredient of their own. But since people were all more or less interested in cooking the same spicy dish, few ingredients were volunteered that would spoil the broth.

Nearer to the march, as difficult, pressing, and pointed decisions had to be made—what went on the banners, in the memorandum, and what should happen at the barricades—the DSF functioned for two or three days as an organization in itself, without recourse to its constituent parts. Mandates were clear; it was now only a question of effecting them. For the most part, old-style comrades who had cut their teeth on the highly charged ideological politics of the seventies and eighties gelled with the younger and newer comrades. By and large the generation gap was productive of energy and innovation. Both sets of people were learning a thing or two from each other. The tediously oblique and hyper-theoretical way of debating points of the past was replaced by a greater informality and an attention to democratic process. The younger comrades, on the other hand, got to witness the old hands wheeling and dealing over resources with the NGO authori-

ties, in the language of these authorities, an essential tactical skill sometimes. Sticking points still presented themselves. The younger generation
felt it necessary to declare on posters and banners, irreverently, "Mbeki is a
poes" (Mbeki is a cunt). Other comrades, mainly from the old school, insisted on dealing only in concepts: "Neo-Liberalism Hurts the Poor."

As the ANC was excluded from the DSF, it tried, in typical fashion, to
disorganize. Their representative at DSF planning meetings in Johannesburg argued for participation in a march celebrating the ANC, warned of
dire consequences should "our government" be embarrassed, flighted stories about international anarchists and terrorists who would be using
marches to create another Genoa, and attacked members of the DSF at a
personal level. But none of these approaches worked. On the day of the DSF
march, with Mbeki being savaged in front of the world's media and a
vibrant new organization just born to challenge the ANC, Michael Sachs
could only stand behind police lines looking confused, his fist involuntari-
ly clenching at his side every time an "Amandla" went up.

If the DSF had a headquarters, it was the Indy Media Centre (IMC) that
was set up during August at the Kingsmead Oval, barely a cricket ball's
throw from the Convention Centre. The IMC meeting room was the prime
venue in the whole stadium overlooking the sports ground on which the
alternative NGO roadshow was being held. Into this space drifted radical
media workers who were part of the European anti-globalization movement, people from the Free Mumia Campaign, activists from a chic North
American outfit called Third World Within,

members of the Dalit People's Movement, and many local South African
lefties attracted to Durban by the NGO conference. Under the say-so of radical former student-leader Prishani Naidoo, now coordinator of the IMC-
South Africa, IMC resources, like computers, telephones, and transport
were free for use by DSF activists. Many accredited IMC media workers
were, in fact, also DSF activists.

IN THE WEEK PRECEDING the official inter-governmental conference,
the NGOs and certain "civil society" organizations working in the area of
race and identity were to be given an opportunity to have their say too.
Marketed self-consciously as a conglomeration at which non-mainstream
or "community voices" could be heard, it attracted the usual array who
earn their keep lobbying, politicking, and gaining public notice for some
or other cause. Many of the causes are noble but many of those speaking on

behalf of these causes are not. The world of NGOs is a cynical yet self-right-eous, populist yet undemocratic, and sympathetic yet disempowering arena. To my mind, the government ministers entering the ICC wearing dark suits appeared no more conformist and dogmatic than the bevy of bleeding-hearts wearing the right T-shirt. It seems, in hindsight, that the alternative conference was mooted precisely as a way of shamming inclu-sion and channeling off anger and heading off mobilization.

Of course, some good people and organizations are forced to play this game and, although preparing mainly for the march, the DSF dabbled in it too. Through the medium of the IMC, they pamphleted in between the stalls of the NGO gathering, convened well-attended press conferences, showed a number of documentaries, and displayed their banners. But most DSF activists remained hostile toward the institution of NGOs. In particu-lar, the bureaucrats of the South African civil society coordinating group, SANGOCO, were openly attacked for their role in attempting to stifle mobi-lization. (This is despite the fact that affiliates of SANGOCO, like the AIDC and Jubilee South, were important members of DSF.) SANGOCO itself was a signed-on member of the DSF. But when SANGOCO officials did attend DSF meetings, it was to try to ensure that the sacrosanct NGO Forum at the Kingsmead Oval was not disrupted in any way. There was so much con-tempt within the DSF for the institution of NGOs that the idea of targeting this conference and ignoring the official and tactically impenetrable UN one was seriously entertained. The DSF engagement with people and organizations at the NGO conference was simply to distinguish the DSF position on racism and poverty from the self-congratulatory position of the South African government as well as from the developmentalist solutions put forward by the majority of NGOs.

The DSF was no homogenous entity, and there were squabbles about allo-cation of money for buses and about the tenor of articles that would appear in the IMC newspaper. The dominance of the discourse around the brutality of the Israeli government against Palestinians threatened to squeeze local demands completely into the background. While no one questioned the need to proclaim support for the second intifada on the terms used by the few peo-ple within the Palestinian Support Group who approached this question from a secular and democratic perspective, the intrusion of South African fundamentalists into DSF activities, such as the planning for the march, was sometimes difficult to handle politely. But in the few days before the march, a solidarity between activists from various DSF constituents had taken hold.

WHEN THE OFFICIAL INTER-GOVERNMENTAL CONFERENCE opened in September, delegates were greeted by three marches. The trade union federation COSATU held theirs on August 30, 2001. Although COSATU is part of the tripartite alliance that, at least rhetorically, rules this country, their march was against a facet of government policy, privatization. It was very measured criticism. Reading their memorandum one could be forgiven for thinking it was all a technical problem that needed to be sorted out between the partners in the alliance and not a fundamental ideological contradiction. It was forgotten that COSATU had initially called for a strike to coincide with the conference, a tactic that would have provided it with enormous leverage. However this strike was never really allowed to happen. ANC top brass pulled out all the stops to avoid "international embarrassment to the president." And so the strike, which would have downed aircraft and disrupted transport and hotels, was downgraded to a well-attended but depressingly lame march on August 30, 2001. Typically, while the mass base of the union federation seem fed up with ANC policy, union bureaucrats were careful not to offend the ANC or the government. This is an especially important consideration as such a high number of unionists eventually get elevated to high office in the state machinery around their fortieth birthdays.

While a few thousand workers joined the DSF march the next day, they did not march as workers. They might have come as members of the community (who also had jobs) or recently retrenched employees who entertained hopes of working again. By and large, though, members of the march were from that class of person who makes up the largest category of South African society, the unemployed 45 percent. Besides publicity in the CCF strongholds themselves and one or two newspaper reports, the assembly was not a general or public one. COSATU didn't publicize the DSF march. Despite repeated attempts by the DSF to get the COSATU regional office to throw in their lot with the DSF, they remained distant and dismissive. The anti-ANC language, uncertainties about the precise legal status of the DSF march, and the loose organizational tenor of the whole thing was out of kilter with the COSATU approach, characterized as it was by always slightly apologetic press statements that accompany marches, long, droning speeches by pompous leaders, and placards that are printed at headquarters beforehand. Their romantic past aside, large bureaucratized COSATU affiliates whose organizational apparatus is geared to national collective bargaining and working the levers of labor law do not have the flexibility, let alone the political will, to be part of actions that encompass a variety of issues and harness a variety of social forces.

The Landless People's Movement contingent as well as a large number of people from the Johannesburg group, Keep Left, arrived on the same day as the COSATU march. Although the latter organization has among its members some fine and committed university-based comrades as well as members of nascent community movements, it suffers the presence of a few self-caricaturing dogmatic Trotskyists ever on the lookout for new recruits to the vanguard. These characters could not patch into the joy and irreverence of it all and aside from making a nuisance of themselves as overzealous marshals on the day of the DSF march, they became invisible.

A dramatic clarification of the cleft between representatives of "civil society" and "civil society" itself occurred when the Johannesburg contingent arrived at the Kingsmead Oval to ask for the assistance of their supposed allies in the NGO movement. Having just alighted from an all-night train trip, they had nowhere to stay. They did not expect to be allowed into the fine hotels where all those involved with the NGO conference were staying, but to be assigned a small patch of land on which to erect tents and shelters. It says a lot that their allies not only declined in horror, but called in the police to have the Johannesburg arrivals dispersed (these people were not accredited and certainly hadn't paid the entrance fee). They eventually found shelter on the grounds of the Natal Technikon where the DSF had hijacked tents erected for another purpose associated with the NGO conference and in which people from the Landless People's Movement had been installed. Quite a festive atmosphere was created at night under these huge tarpaulin shelters, closed on three sides, where Durban's famous bunny-chow meals were served for free but the beer had to be bought.

The next day was the DSF march. In banner-painting sessions, the CCF desire to have a no-holds-barred activity the next day prevailed. This would not be a conceptual rejection of capitalism or neoliberalism but a direct attack on the agents of anti-poor policies in this country—the ANC. Speakers who would say this were put on the speakers list.

From early in the morning of August 31, 2001, buses assembled in townships across Durban. In Mpumalanga and Kwa-Mashu the night before, a few ANC loyalists had gone around these townships alternatively threatening people not to support the DSF march or sowing disinformation, saying the DSF march had been postponed until the next day. Despite this, people arrived in their thousands. Event organizers could hardly believe the size of the crowd that stood assembled at nine o'clock on the grounds of the Natal Technikon. The Landless, the Chatsworth communities, the Soweto electricity people, the Cape Town Anti-Eviction Campaign, the Palestinian Supporters, students from the University of Durban-Westville, the Treatment Action Campaign.

IT IS DIFFICULT TO CAPTURE the joy and surprise and vibrancy of the march. Snaking its way through the streets of Durban over a seven kilometer course, it was the largest public demonstration seen in the city since the anti-apartheid marches of days gone by. Estimates in the mainstream press put the march at between 20,000 to 30,000 strong. As I have never been able to estimate the size of a march, I will stick to that figure. Some of the folk we have met during the course of this book where there. Sipho Mlaba, who is a portly fellow, was sweating. He had walked up and down the outsides of the march a few times, making sure all the Mpumalangan youth were together and ready for his signal to jog quickly to the front of the march just as it reached its end outside the ICC. They were anxious to confront Thabo Mbeki, who their slogans identified as a source of their misery.

Cosmos Desmond and Dennis Brutus walked, sage-like, together at the back of the march, two immensely respected figures whose association with the DSF had given its activities a certain struggle respectability. Pinky Naidoo, husband of Orlean, wore his familiar cap and dark glasses and he too was somewhere near the back of the crowd. You might remember Shoba, the young woman from Chatsworth. She and Thulisile Manqele shared an umbrella. Virginia Setshedi of the SECC was sitting on the back of a flat-bed truck on which the public address system was conveyed. She led the chants, which alternated between condemning the policies and condemning the purveyors thereof: "Phansi privatization, Phansi! Away with Mbeki's AIDS Genocide, Away."

Anna Weekes, prominent Anti-Eviction Campaign member and also a COSATU affiliate official was in amongst the Mpumalangans. She and Ishmael Peterson of Tafelsig wore homemade T-Shirts denouncing privatization. Trevor Ngwane of the SECC, who is also a well-known anti-corporate globalization campaigner in the United States, loped along for a while next to Richard Pithouse, a university lecturer and writer. Both are tall, with long hair and are striking in appearance. I heard them laughing loudly at a joke Trevor likes to tell (and forgets he already has) about capitalism explained to a child.

When the front of the march reached the police cordon about two hundred meters from the ICC, there was a pause in proceedings as the back of the march was allowed to catch up and Muslim marchers turned to Mecca to say their prayers. Meanwhile, the government sent a low-ranking official to receive the memorandum as the entire interchange of Old Fort and Stanger Roads filled up with bodies. There was no platform or stage for the leaders of this march. A small space around the truck in the center of the march was maintained with people surrounding this space all around like a doughnut. One felt part of this mass, able to participate and influence its movements. Next, Fatima Meer took the microphone and read out the DSF Declaration, an excoriating indictment of the right-wing slide of a government that still had the audacity to parade as a liberation movement. The LPM memorandum was no less clear. It called for the scrapping of the property clause in the constitution and the acceleration of land redistribution. Its language damned the Mbeki regime for its pandering to the interests of big commercial farmers and yoking other forms of redistribution to the power of tribal chiefs, the very policies of British rule in South Africa. While these ceremonies took place, some Mpumalangan, University of Durban-Westville, and Wits University activists breached the police line of huge concrete blocks. The police seemed to have relied on these to keep the crowd at bay for there were suddenly only two lines of them between an angry crowd and the ICC. They lowered their helmets and braced their shields.

After the last speaker had finished talking, a cry went up, "ICC! ICC!" Those in the front wanted to cross the police line. The world should see, in the violent rejection of its authority, how much the poor of South Africa despised the government that ruled in their name. Why had Mbeki shown such disrespect by not accepting the memo himself or sending a cabinet minister, at least, to do so? If he would not come to them, they would fetch him from the Hilton Hotel. Setshedi took the microphone and scolded government for sending such a low-ranking official. The masses had been patient. Next time they would not. A toyi-toyi song that heaped scorn on Mbeki went up. The marchers advanced, then retreated, then advanced on the police-line again. This had suddenly become too much for Abie Dithlake, the senior SANGOCO bureaucrat on hand, who might have realized that he was standing in the full glare of dozens of TV cameras at the head of a march denouncing the most powerful man in South African politics. He put up his hands to stop the song. It became louder. He shouted, then screeched into the microphone for the march to turn around and disperse to a venue not far away. Some people complied. Most did not. The cry of "ICC! ICC!" was resuscitated. Others told Dithlake to "Voetsek!" Professor Meer too had her attempts to move the crowd away bluntly rejected. Who was she? A phalanx of protestors rushed toward the police. Suddenly a metal gate that had been found (who knows where) was thrown toward the police line and used as a battering ram. A scuffle broke out. The police grabbed the gate. More revolutionary songs were sung, loud and fast, the footfalls and claps of the toyi-toyi sounding like gun shots. Dithlake and other SANGOCO functionaries made haste towards Hoy Park. A large rump of the crowd remained behind. One of the Trotskyist members of Keep Left who proudly wore a yellow armband proclaiming him "Chief Marshal" went to the front of the crowd. He yelled that people must obey him. The march was over, they should go back. To make his point, he singled out a young and militant student leader from Wits who was part of those keen to, at least, threaten the storming of the ICC for a while longer. Grabbing his T-shirt and pushing against his chest, the Chief Marshal cried "Move Back." The guys from Mpumalanga and UDW student leaders Prava Pillay and Xolani Shange would have none of this. I will not dwell on what happened next, but the Chief Marshal of the march, found himself on the floor in an instant, nursing sore ribs and broken lips for the rest of the week.   The intra-DSF fight discouraged quite a number of those willing to storm the barricades but not fight with each other. One of the coordinators of the LPM contingent declared that "our people are not ready for this direct action yet." He led most of this huge part of the march away. Other DSF militants also took stock, perhaps with the controversies of Genoa in their heads, and drifted to Hoy Park. There was no longer a critical mass of protestors to sustain a charge and so, reluctantly, after another half hour or so of talk and dance and celebration, they too joined the meeting already under way at Hoy Park.

AFTER THE FRACAS AT THE BARRICADES and the handing out of the memorandum, the crowd had come in batches to Hoy Park, not far from the ICC. Here various speakers had their say. Someone from the Free Mumia Abu Jamal campaign spoke. So too did a representative of the Dalits movement in India and a remarkable youngster from the refugee camps of the Gaza Strip. Respected U.S. academic, Manning Marable, also said a few words, reflecting on the continued intermingling of race and poverty not only in Africa but elsewhere in the African diaspora.

Mangaliso Kubheka, a spokesperson for the Kwa-Zulu-Natal offshoot of the LPM, drew rapturous applause when he said the movement's members were prepared to die for their cause and that they had been betrayed by President Thabo Mbeki. "The very president who we voted for is pointing fingers at us. He was sitting in London while we knew the smell of tear gas in our fight to get rid of apartheid." The CCF message was very short. It challenged those who were serious about opposing poverty and inequality in South Africa to have the courage to admit that this now meant fighting against the ANC. Despite the hurly-burly nature of the march and its anti-climactic end, most people left in good spirits. With all its warts and blemishes, something new had been born.

Some in the media did not fail to notice the challenge implicit in the three marches. The following excerpts are from an article in the Durban *Sunday Tribune*:

> COSATU, the Durban Social Forum (DSF) and the ANC all organized marches to coincide with the opening of the World Conference Against Racism. The DSF march, which was over 20,000 strong was by far the largest and the most militant of the three marches. Much of the reporting on the DSF has failed to understand that it was a decisive moment in the history of post-apartheid South Africa. For the first time there was a mass based and very public rejection of the ANC, their economic policies and the leadership of Thabo Mbeki.
>
> Marchers, most of whom had funded their trip to the march themselves, carried home-made banners and posters with slogans like "Mbeki is a Liar," "ANC is an Agent of Global Apartheid," " Stop the Assault on the Poor—Reverse GEAR," and "Mbeki, AIDS is as Real as cANCer." Thousands of marchers wore headbands reading "Durban Social Forum Says Phansi GEAR." The DSF was the coming out of a new force in South African politics and society . . . This loose collection of community based social movements united by their opposition to the ANC's policies is now a significant force in South African politics.

THE ANC MARCH was held the next day, September 1, 2001. Despite having an unlimited transport budget, according to press reports only 5,000 to 10,000 people arrived, many of them schoolchildren. Many of these disembarked from the buses and promptly caught mini-bus taxis to the beach. How the governing party that is implementing policies that pauperize

people, deny mothers affordable AIDS drugs, evict the indigent, and cut off
their access to services while creating an environment where the rich accu-
mulate even greater wealth, dares to hazard a march for human rights can
only be explained by this organization's incredible ability to mystify. Strad-
dling the official and the grassroots, the regime and the people, the rich
and the poor, this organization still commands pockets of emotional support (and rather larger pockets of electoral support). However, as its betrayal of the poor becomes more and more profound, this support inexorably
flows away, month by month.

Perhaps Angela Davis was caught up in this mystification, for she was
part of the ANC march and gave it her support. Perhaps it was a Communist Party hangover that did it, or the attitude that Africans find so comical
in some of their transatlantic sisters and brothers: the desperately uncriti-
cal need to be vaunted and affirmed by those holding power and title back
in Mother Africa. One APF member commented that marching with ANC
bigshots for "the hopes and dreams of a better life for Black people is like
marching with J. Edgar Hoover for civil rights."

If Davis and others had acted in the belief that the ANC was still a force
for liberation in a global order dominated by Western imperialism, their
hopes were betrayed by the shameful conduct of the ANC within the inter-
governmental conference. Rather than presenting any diplomatic leadership on the issues that it was uniquely placed to provide, it mollycoddled
the Western nations, seeking a compromise that would prevent any clear
position from being taken on the burning issues of reparations for colonialism and slavery and the Israeli occupation of Palestine. It seemed their
thinking was that the conference had to adopt some resolution, no matter
how watered down, or otherwise the host nation's future as a conference
center would be drawn into question. The walkout by the United States
drew only the most craven of "regrets."

Within South Africa, the conference had a very different significance.
To some outside observers it might have confirmed the symbolic role of the
ANC in global struggles against oppression, but for the oppressed in South
Africa it was an opportunity to create the first radical national organ of the
"Left" since 1994: the DSF. For the first time a mass of people had mobilized
against the ANC government. The DSF built concrete links between
activists from many different areas and traditions; so much so that something solid has remained behind months after Durban. It gave the people
involved in the Tafelsig, Mpumalanga, Isipingo, Soweto, and Chatsworth a

sense that there were experiences and moods out there in the country that corresponded to their own. Most importantly, it validated a form of collectivity, the community movements, free from the ideological inhibitions of organized labor or the tired dogmas of the Left.

18. building a movement?

We do not believe in Buthelezi's Zulu nation
or Mbeki's Renaissance for Africans. We believe in free basic
services for all poor people. This we need for life.
We believe in life. That is why we organize with the people
of Chatsworth and show solidarity with the land appropriators
of Bredell and the Soweto Electricity Crisis Committee.

—MANDLA GWALA, union organizer and civic leader, Mpumalanga

I THINK OF ANNELINE GANESH'S FRAGILE BODY ran over by a hundred frightened kids at the Throb nightclub in Chatsworth in March 2000, her side ripped open and her leg hanging limp. She is a prisoner of her third floor flat. She was abandoned by her father at birth. Her mother, Sherene, toils in the clothing industry. But if the clothing industry continues its trajectory of shedding jobs, Sherene will be condemned to unemployment. Anneline does not realize that soon her family will be involved in a struggle to hold onto her little prison room.

I think about Emanuel Mhlongo who longs to bring up his family in Unit 2 in Chatsworth. I think about his quiet dignity and backbreaking work to keep his family together. I think about all those Indian "aunties" who braved live ammunition to stave off his eviction. The reporters kept asking them about the fact he was African. Most of the aunties could not relate to the question because they could only see a neighbor. But Mhlongo will find less and less work as a bush mechanic and will probably eventually lose his house.

I think about Mrs Anamuthoo at the age of 81. She survived but her son will not. He will never raise the capital to get his sewing machine back. The indefinite short-time from the footwear factory will be precisely that—indefinite—for the imports will keep flooding in.

I think about the post-apartheid trials of Thulisile Manqele whose water Judge Viven Niles-Duner has ordered to be disconnected again, mainly because she was not disciplined enough to turn her neighbors away when they came begging for a bucketful.

I think about the writings evaluating Mbeki's presidency and the new South Africa. Such balanced appraisal, and so clever. But if he has not unleashed it, then he is presiding over economic genocide. Unemployment has spiraled and in a rampant market economy this is a death sentence. A medical specialist tells me that the annual budget for the oncology unit at the King Edward hospital is R60,000. Enough for one patient. Beds at the state hospitals are being closed down all the time. Happiness Shinga and her daughter wait to die. The AZT provided to raped tourists is too expensive for them. More prisons are being built. More youth from Chatsworth will find a bed there. Fewer houses. More evictions. The minister of finance, Trevor Manuel, does not assess the deficit to the poor when he reads his budget speech in his cute, silk polka-dot tie.

I go to a May Day rally organized by COSATU. Geraldine-Fraser Moleketi, a member of the central committee of the South African Communist Party with a distinctly Margaret Thatcher hairstyle, is guest speaker. As minister of social welfare she forgot to spend R198 million on the poor, and she slashed the child-care grant to needy parents by three-quarters. The economy of entire villages has been wiped out by this decision of hers. She is now minister of public enterprises, and has the task of holding down wages and eliminating jobs in the public service.

Images of powerful women in parliament are scarred by the memories of a meeting of women in Unit 10, Chatsworth, who had just had their child maintenance grant cutoff. Some had taken their children out of school using them instead as begging tools. Some just wept. How can women just be expected to pick up the slack when these kinds of decisions are made? I know there are women in high places, but it is difficult to see policies implemented with such callousness without suspecting misogyny. The South African Constitution provides for permanent commissions to oversee human rights and matters related to gender. But I hesitate to tell them about these commissions knowing that approaching these toothless bodies will lead to more disappointment.

I am haunted by the body bags outside the Throb and the white-gloved mortuary workers who, like the Poles in Hamlet, pick up the bodies, seemingly oblivious to the events that went before. I know that this "tragedy" is a singular event and unusual. But is this an omen of what the future holds, or perhaps a chance, graphic presentation of what is happening already today, privately, behind the doors where the poors live?

The struggles that began in Chatsworth and spread from there reveal much about the transition to democracy in South Africa. So often they are aimed at no more than remaining in dilapidated accommodation devoid of basic social amenities, without lights and water. And yet they are seen as a threat to the state. The poor are having to fight to remain ensconced in the ghettoes to which apartheid consigned them. Are these the revolutionary demands we make?

But in Chatsworth and elsewhere, communities are organizing and fighting back. They have developed networks of communication among the different units and interdependent relationships with lawyers, academics, human rights groups and journalists on the outside. Led mainly by women, many of whose biographies tell a story of abuse that once cowered them into submission, they have reemerged to take on a new bully-boy— the local government.

TAKING ON LOCAL GOVERNMENT is in itself no more than an interim measure, a necessary defense against forces that will renew their attacks on the poor. The forms of solidarity that enable poor people to stand together against evictions and cutoffs are not necessarily sufficient to change the system that keeps them impoverished. But it is a starting-point for building a larger movement, and these actually existing collectivities are a more concrete starting-point for building that movement than any academic analysis or abstract set of principles.

What are the principles that hold these communities together in their struggles? At a big rally in Mpumalanga during the WCAR, there was righteous anger expressed at the thought of forcing people to pay for water. "Water comes from God, it is needed for life," was the constant refrain. After the Battle of Bayview, when Jooma was interviewed for Ben Cashdan's SABC *Special Assignment* documentary, he kept saying, "We are not animals, we are human beings." This is all the ideology one gets a moment after Jooma has been shot by police while trying to prevent the eviction of his neighbor, Emmanuel Mhlongo.

Both he and the crowd in Mpumalanga hold expectations of a certain level of material needs fulfillment and they expect to be treated as if they possess "human rights." These expectations, in my experience, are rooted within the struggles and day-to-day experiences of poor people like him in all the communities we have passed through in this book. Unlike the macroeconomists—on the left and right alike—the poors are not flummoxed with talk of (no) alternatives or being realistic. It is striking that the actual demands of people are almost always within what is possible, what can be achieved. The problem is—it won't be given or it is busy being taken away. This is the power these community movements have. They can "realistically" achieve their immediate goals but only through struggle. It is, I think, in light of these two factors—the expectation of a certain level of social good and the sense that it is being deliberately withheld or taken away—that people are willing to resist the UniCity's demand for payment. And in so doing there is an actual and cumulative disruption of the logic of capital and not a mere dispute with it no matter how comprehensively footnoted.

Of absolutely crucial importance is that is no insistence that resistance should assume a character significantly different from the expectations that inform it. People are not being prevailed upon to involve themselves in party politics or to march against tariff barrier reductions or adopt the ideology of Black Consciousness, as valuable as any of these activities might be in the broader scheme of things. A totally new political sensibility is developing that is neither attentive to the inner workings of the World Bank nor, for that matter, intimidated by these institutions or overwhelmed by the distance between the poors and these enemies. Indeed, from the vantage point of the poors, reforms in these arenas are not possible, nor are they particularly desirable.

On the other hand, news of social struggles in Soweto, Zimbabwe, Bolivia, and Genoa communicated, for example, in workshops run by the SECC's wonderful Virginia Setshedi, shown on TV, or spoken about at meetings, are received with intense interest and joy. These struggles are somehow very near, almost local, and inspiringly winnable. This attention given to every practical possibility of struggle and the making local of certain global issues is an incredible antidote to the paralysis felt in the official left at the prospects of social change.

Because of how close the demands advanced are to "reality," people are not willing to go to inordinate lengths to earn an income to satisfy the Council's demand for payment. They will rather struggle to win demands that are achievable. While unemployment is incredibly high, it is notionally possible for women in Chatsworth to find a job in the myriad of backyard sweatshops that have recently sprung up, but as long as they are able to put food on the table, few bother to make the extra effort that would enable them to meet these payments. Similarly, only a tiny percentage of those too poor to pay their water bills in Mpumalanga present themselves as sexm workers at the Truck-Stops. People who have a few rands extra each month do not voluntarily hand it over to the UniCity in lieu of arrears. They would rather spend it on something they want. It is mainly people like Shoba of Chatsworth who, in order to escape some very private nightmare, submit to a sweatshop regime in order to scrape together every small bit of cash and thus some personal relief.

The majority just stay put. And this staying put is often not seen as the remarkably active event that it is. The DSF-style of politics has revealed the importance of not seeing the poors only as victims as many on the South African left tend to do. Their "consuming services" for which they do not pay has cost the UniCity dearly at a number of levels. Not only has the UniCity lost millions of dollars in revenue but their awe as an authority capable of exerting themselves has been dented in other areas where people are not quite ready to resist—as yet. This brings home the point that resistance does not always take the highly visible form of marches. Nonpayment and the refusal to perform ultra-exploitative wage labor is preeminently a form of resistance.

So is the communal cooking and sharing we have seen in Chatsworth and Mpumalanga. The meeting venues and assemblage points are invested with a power of their own. "Road 332" (Westcliff), "the deadend" (Bayview), "under the tree" (Woodhurst), "Sishi's Store" (Mpumalanga), "The Hall" (Wentworth) are places synonymous with struggle. People's faces are connected with brave and daring events, like Jooma's bullet, Jane Smith's bag of badges, and Sipho Mlaba's sugar-beans.

Not all, but large numbers of people in the communities come into contact with each other in totally new relationships. At night people escape the loneliness and lethargy of TV or slumber to crisscross their areas bearing messages or pamphlets or gossip. After visiting Chatsworth with a comrade from Johannesburg, Franco Barchiesi, and while enjoying a meal at Durban's best eating spot, Little Gujerat, I was struck by his comment about how "sensuous" the lived environment of the poors actually was. I had not put my own finger on what was so different about working in these areas before. This was it: the capacity to sense collective joy (and also misery) seemed heightened here in comparison to other "sites of struggle," like the factory.

THE QUESTION of the politics of the movement that is growing out of these struggles was most clearly evident in the formation of the Durban

Social Forum. The formation of the DSF at the need to respond to the South African government's hosting of the World Conference Against Racism also forced activists to discuss political questions more fully, and raised the question of whether this broader political sensibility could become a commonly held ideological position.

DSF activists working within the IMC did not try to be the mouthpiece for a left view. Although not fully or consistently emerging as such, the DSF was a space and a set of practices beyond the Left. Here people who had inhabited radical subjectivities in the past that had fragmented and left them disheartened, once again entered the mass political realm, trying new languages and ideas. They now felt that they were part of a new form of politics, but the nature of that politics was still under discussion.

I remember sitting outside the IMC suite one night during the WCAR, high up above the cricket pitch. The stadium spotlights cast a pearly glow over the tents below, between which scurried NGO workers, all carrying different colored bags slung across their shoulders. After a minute of staring, it looked like the bags were the animate objects and the human carriers the mere appendages. Some other DSF participants, resting after a stint of late night work, also occupied these best seats in the house. There was agreement that while left values were still important to us, the left project often took on forms that became an obstacle to realizing those values. This was true at least to the extent that left organizations are based on a mere philosophy of domination that confines social subjects to the role of either passive victims who, at best, are defeated spontaneists or else are card-carrying cadres of the revolutionary party. The left has been unable to recognize the teeming life in between. Life! This is not just a theoretical issue. The practice of left organization in South Africa had become so disconnected from the dreams, desires, and emotions of ourselves and the people among whom we had moved these last few years as to be completely ineffective.

It may have had its historical moment but the Left's ways of relating to everyday life in Chatsworth, Mpumalanga, and Tafelsig, is now inadequate, I found myself thinking. If I was a traditional leftist, I would have to spend all my time first engineering the content of the life of people in these communities so that it accorded with the insights of socialism. That would be the struggle! But this is not the way things are. There is a rich, complex, imperfect, and sensuous collectivity existing in the communities I have written about. And the way certain of these needs are expressed and stubbornly held onto as the basis for action is not frowned upon by people in the DSF as it is, even if secretly, by many socialists.

There are dangers, of course. Talk of human rights and citizenship often results in validation of the social order. It is also tempting to use the processes for adjudication of disputes precisely in this realm, like the courts, provided by the system. When one wins in these forums, it is easy to vaunt the rule of law but then what happens when you need to break it? Parochialism, too, has to be warded off and efforts made to be sensitive to the struggles of other subaltern groups. But there is no doubt for me that whatever the dangers, there would be little civic resistance at all today in South Africa if it was not for expectations of dignity, human rights and a dignified life in the terms noted above.

I tried to say some of these things to my comrades sitting next to me. Perhaps they were simply humoring me, but one or two nodded gravely when I stopped. After a while someone ventured another reason why the notion of the Left could no longer be safely employed. It was too all-embracing. This was particularly obvious when one considered the hypocrisy of the NGO "sector". It was not the content of the criticism of government policy that mattered. Anyone could say they were against racism and poverty or recite socialist principles without presenting the least bit of a challenge. Witness the SACP. Increasingly, it was the unassimilable form in which demands for change and desires for life that were put across that was important in defining who was friend or foe. From this point of view, calls to unify the Left were dangerous.

Another comrade told a story about a young man who was part of Operation Khanyisa, the illegal electricity reconnection project in Johannesburg townships. He failed to make a number of community meetings. When he returned, she asked him where he had been. In a perfectly matter-of-fact way he had\said, "Oh, I'm sorry, my sister needed to go to school so I decided to try crime for a while." His opposition to neoliberalism was not evinced in carefully footnoted academic tracts but in his willingness, amongst other things, to manhandle the Eskom security guards who come into his area to effect disconnections. The former leftist the system actually encouraged, the latter it could not take. It was with people like the young man that she said she could join hands.

FOR MANY OF THE ACTIVISTS at the core of these groups, working in different spaces and having different strategies and tactics, there was one binding thread. There was unmitigated opposition to the economic policies adopted by the ANC. Again and again DSF activists spoke of how the right-wing economic policies lead to widespread and escalating unemployment, with concomitant water and electricity cutoffs, and evictions even from the "toilets in the veld" provided by the government in the place of houses. More importantly there was general agreement that this was not just a question of short-term pain for long-term gain. The ANC had become a party of neoliberalism. The strategy to win the ANC to a left project was a dead end. The ANC had to be challenged and a movement built to render its policies unworkable. It seems increasingly unlikely that open confrontation with the repressive power of the post-apartheid state can be avoided.

Events taking place as this book goes to press show that such confrontation is already beginning. On Saturday, April 6, 2002, about 100 residents of Soweto gathered at the Funda Center, and set off to protest electricity and water disconnections. Residents were particularly incensed because Johannesburg mayor Amos Masondo has failed to honor a promise to write off half the arrears of people who paid R25 a month; a sum of money many people could ill afford but had nevertheless been paying. Thirty-seven of the protestors were pensioners whose main fear was the approaching Highveld winter which would see temperatures dropping on some nights to below zero. In line with a favored tactic of the new community movements of confronting the actual politician or bureaucrat who caused their misery, the busses threaded their way through the dusty Soweto streets, over a thirty kilometer concrete highway and then disappeared beneath the canopy of trees that lined the posh Johannesburg suburb of Kensington where Mayor Amos Masondo lives.

The protest was initially peaceful. The small crowd sang songs outside Masondo's sprawling mansion. Then suddenly Masondo's bodyguard appeared on the roof. He pointed his firearm at those singing and let loose firing no less than 8 rounds of live ammunition into the crowd which scattered. Some of the young men among the crowd lobbed clods of earth and small stones in his direction in an effort to provide some time for the very young and old to get some cover. Two people, Aubrey Batji and Samson Khumalo were shot, luckily receiving only flesh wounds. Samson Khumalo's circumstance mirrored that of most of the crowd. He supported his wife and five grandchildren on his R570 pension. He told the Sunday Times that "This government promised a good life, but there isn't any" (7 April 2002).

By now a part of the crowd had regrouped and were incensed. While the bodyguard still trained his weapon on the people below and as the first sirens of approaching police cars made themselves heard, a small posse of boys dived into Masondo's garden and with a manhole cover expertly lifted, they disconnected the Mayor's water supply before rushing back to their comrades outside the gates.

The police arrested all of the protesters on charges of malicious damage to property and public violence. The bodyguard was asked to report to the police station and was released immediately. The protestors were destined for a different reception at the police station. The size of the police contingent should have alerted the SECC to what was coming. It was so huge and staffed by such senior officials, that it was clear their "crimes" had been politicized. Kept in the Jeppe police station cells over the weekend, it was expected that all would be granted bail on the Monday. But the authorities clearly wanted to make an example of the SECC activists. They were helped in this by an SACP stalwart and upholder of law and order against the revolting working class. Although he had been part of the march, he now enthusiastically joined the police in identifying protestors. He pointed out a member of the SECC legal team who went to the police-station to bring blankets and food. She was promptly arrested. The police officers said they would make a point of bringing them to Court so late that even if they were released it would be too late for the pensioners among the group to receive their monthly pension payouts due on the Monday. Then the police allegedly ran out of stationery with which to process those who were arrested who were therefore left standing for hours and hours in lines.

By Monday morning, the prosecuting authorities had a new trick up their sleeve. Except in the case of a few people, the senior State prosecutor brought in to try these relatively minor offences, vigorously opposed granting bail. The supposed reason for this was that it had not been possible to verify the addresses of most of those arrested. This was a ridiculous assertion. Many among the SECC were well-known people and the police hardly had to rely on an address to track down the likes of Trevor Ngwane or Rob Rees, a prominent South African Municipal Workers' Union organizer. But the Magistrate accepted these improbable arguments and Ngwane, Rees and the rest of the SECC group were remanded in custody until April 16, 2002. They were ordered to be kept in South Africa's equivalent of San Quentin Penetentiary, the notorious Diepkloof prison, amongst hardened criminals and the cruellest of wardens. On April 16 the detainees appeared at the Jeppe Magistrates court. The *Mercury*, KZN's leading morning daily

reported the unfolding events: "Hundreds of Soweto protestors made fires
on the steps of the Jeppe Magistrate court and burned their ANC membership cards as part of the anti-privatization protests which gained momentum countrywide. In a show of solidarity, a picket was mounted outside the
Magistrate's Court in Durban by the Concerned Citizen's Forum. Similar
action was organized in other centers in the country" (April 17, 2002). The
50 who were arrested were released and asked to appear in court on May 10.

Clearly a clampdown on South Africa's emerging community movement has been signaled. The only question is whether these movements
will be crushed by such repression or deflected into ineffectual forms of
struggle or whether this will harden their resolve and bestow upon
activists the dignity of sacrifice and the glory of struggling for what is
right. Will the ANC's turning on the poor solidify the combativeness and
inventiveness of the community movements as it, itself, was once strengthened by apartheid oppression?

MUCH REMAINS UNDECIDED. But a movement is growing in South
Africa, quietly encroaching upon the State prerogatives to charge for the
"privilege" of living. Rooted in communities and with an ideology, if that is
the right word, that springs from ideas of neighborliness, dignity, and life,
these movements proffer winnable demands which they pursue with considerable imagination and vigor. If the response of the South African government is anything to go by, these movements are proving fairly effective.
They are wary of the ideological archaism of the ultra-left and the desperation of pure protest. They have raised, but not yet answered, the question of
what organization/s will best serve the growing dissent to the right-wing
ANC and facilitate more sustained outright rebellion. Perhaps there is no
traditional organizational way.

These community movements seem to be finding a way through the
paralysis of either getting bogged down in the damp and passionless dogmas of the hitherto existing Left or buying into class compromise in some
way. Only a few years after "national liberation," they are developing a
form of class politics, but imbued with passions beyond left politics. This
movement has a world-historical sense of itself but focuses on combat with
local enemies and thrives on small victories. We are at that precarious
point in South African history where something precious and powerful is
coming into being. To report the existence of this growing movement of
the poors of South Africa has been the task of this book.

appendix:
durban social forum declaration

THIS DECLARATION was adopted at a mass meeting of the Durban Social Forum held in the township of Mpumalanga on August 28, 2001. The DSF was created to organize a response to South Africa's hosting the UN World Conference Against Racism. Its declaration is a message of solidarity with oppressed people around the world. The original declaration was drafted and adopted in isiZulu, and translated into English.

IT HAS BEEN SEVEN YEARS since apartheid ended in the country where we live. It has been seven years since the open wound of colonialism was finally stitched closed on the continent of Africa. The defeat of political systems which for over 350 years created so much human degradation and racial violence against Africans, brought a moment of hope and a moment of rest for many of us who live below the Limpopo River. By 1994 the tireless exertions of the workers, the militance of the people in the townships, as well as the sacrifices of the gallant youth during the 1980s, finally had brought down the white-minority government. In the process, we had built strong, democratic organizations and elected individuals to lead us whom we trusted as honest and principled people. Of course, we still had to start building a new society ourselves. But we looked to our leaders for policies that would make this possible by redistributing the wealth held by a tiny group of families and corporations in South Africa. Who could blame us for wanting to beat our swords into ploughshares?

For a while we really hoped things would get better, even though we kept being told of delays and compromises and new economic plans to satisfy the West. We thought, "If not for us, then for our children." But things started to go wrong. The important people—increasingly just appointed to lead us—we knew them not. Before elections they spoke many fine words, but by their deeds we saw that they no longer cared about us. When we looked around, we saw that many of our leaders had not struggled for freedom with us or suffered like we had. And even those who had been with us, started keeping their distance. We read the soft words they spoke to the rich men in our country, and soon we heard the harsh words they began speaking to us.

We were told to pay money or be thrown out of our homes, to pay school-fees or have our children prevented from learning. We were told that without money we would be given no water or lights and minimal medical care. They gave this an indigenous name, Masakhane, to pretend that they acted for our own good. But all the while, jobs were being cut by the hundred thousand and there was no money coming into our communities anymore. One day we woke up to learn that it was now the Government's actual policy to lose jobs, to cut off the water of the indigent, to reduce child-care grants by half, and to evict with violence those who could not pay for a piece of land or a roof over their heads. Most shocking, as hospitals and clinics were closed down all over the countryside, we were told that "our" government would refuse us medicine for HIV/AIDS, even when it could prevent babies being infected by this terrible plague.

The leaders became unrecognizable to us. Even physically. They became bloated with gravy and their faces distorted behind the dark glass of their luxury cars. They seemed to be much happier overseas groveling in front of world leaders when, not long ago, we had all shared an understanding that it was the powerful in the West and the North that had an interest in our exploitation.

We are sad to report that, since 1999, things have become very bad in this country for Black people and the poor. The policies this regime is pursuing have caused outbreaks of serious diseases like cholera. Half of all Black children in rural areas go hungry every day and, although a few Black people in the upper echelons of the ANC have become fantastically wealthy, South Africa now has the greatest divide between rich and poor of any country in the world. Our President's arrogance and cowardice have caused thousands of preventable AIDS deaths. The police shoot dead students again who protest against unaffordable fees and the closing down of unprofitable departments. Instead of a solution to the land hunger of our people, we have evictions of families living on land stolen from their forefathers, carried out with a brutality we never thought we would live to see again.

And so, reluctantly at first but now with a deepening fury, communities have started to resist. In Chatsworth and Mpumalanga in KwaZulu Natal, bloody battles have been fought against evictions and water cutoffs. The

same has happened in Tafelsig on the Cape Flats. And in Bredell in Gauteng, landless people seized their birthright. They were defeated, but will
always be remembered as the beginning of a movement for radical redistribution of land, away from those who do not need it and towards those who
are desperate for any piece they can get. In Isipingo, the community has
voted out of office all political parties, and elected instead a local council
member directly accountable to them. In Soweto, people are trained to
reconnect electricity and water and occupy the smart offices of the companies that urge service cutoffs. In Johannesburg, an anti-privatization
group, which unites comrades from many different traditions of activism,
is growing from strength to strength.

These local community struggles have shone a light not only by their
courage in the face of the enemy, but also courage in the face of our own
prejudices. It is supremely ironic, and tragic, that this government's policies continue to barricade the poor into racial ghettoes to fight over neoliberalism's crumbs while a few of the rulers share out the loot. The result,
increasingly, is the creation of race hate. Nonetheless, our courage can free
us. For example, in this city of Durban where colonial rulers encouraged
divisions between Indian, coloured and African people, a sense of non-
racialism is defiantly entrenched in the community organizations as we
confront our common lot not as separate races, but as "the poors."

Recently, we have come to understand more about the "global village,"
and are ashamed about the role our government has chosen to play as an
induna of the West. We wish to apologize to the people of Palestine, Harlem,
East Timor, Congo, Chiapas, Algeria, Burma, Sudan, Iraq, the Dalits of
India, the workers in Asian sweatshops, the women downtrodden in
Afghanistan, the street-children in Sao Paulo, the political prisoners in the
United States, the villagers in the Maluti Mountain Valley, the Aborigines
in Australia, the immigrants of Europe and North America, and every
other place in our world where injustice is perpetuated while the leaders
of our country keep conveniently quiet, or even support your oppressors.
We are learning about economic globalization too. We realize that while
some wounds from the past have been sewn shut, many others have been
torn open—on the body of the earth and on the bodies of human beings.
Colonialism is dead but new overlords impose themselves. The World Bank,
WEF, G8, IMF, and WTO. They are supported not only by lackey governments like our own but also by a legion of other forked-tongue abbrevia-
tions: NGOs, UNOs, USAIDs, and WCARs, of which we are all deeply

suspicious, despite their pretense at caring for us.

But we don't despair. We are encouraged by what we have read, heard on the radio, or seen on TV, about how our brothers and sisters in the North are bravely struggling to determine the character of the new world economy. Their ways of struggling are at once so different and so similar to ours. As our struggles merge, we are going to learn better and stronger ways of fighting against those who hurt us. We will not make the mistakes of the past, when all too often we trusted leaders or parties or nations or races to save us. We know now that only the freedom and justice we the people build together, has the strength to resist oppression.